Stitch style

20 Fashion Knit and Crochet Patterns

Bags

COLLINS & BROWN

Introduction

The latest in the successful collection of **Stitch Style** books, **Stitch Style Bags** features a collection of ultimately desirable knitted and crocheted bags – from chunky satchels to classy evening bags; from giant, on-trend handbags to casual and colourful totes. Whether you're a college girl or an urban professional, carry only the bare essentials or like to lug your life around with you, the bag you want and need is in this book.

Designed by fashion-loving knitters for crafting soulmates, all the bags have straightforward instructions, stylish photography and a skill level, so there's something for you whether you're a novice or a yarn supremo.

Choose your first project, take a delicious trip to your LYS and buy the ideal yarn – and possibly a few other irresistible balls for your stash – brush up on techniques with a glance at the back of the book, and let your fingers fly making your perfect bag; the first of many perfect bags you are going to want to make from **Stitch Style Bags**.

stitch*style*
Bags

First published in the UK in 2009 by
Collins & Brown
10 Southcombe Street
London
W14 0RA

An imprint of Anova Books Company Ltd

Distributed in the United States and Canada by
Sterling Publishing Co, 387 Park Avenue South,
New York, NY 10016, USA

ISBN 978-1-84340-487-3

A CIP catalogue for this book is available from
the British Library.

10 9 8 7 6 5 4 3 2 1

Photography by Rebecca Maynes
Illustrations by Kang Chen

Reproduction by Rival Colour Ltd, UK
Printed and bound by NPE Print Communication
Pte Ltd, Singapore

This book can be ordered direct from the
publisher. Contact the marketing department, but
try your bookshop first.

www.anovabooks.com

Contents

DESIGNED BY

Gosia Dzik-Holden

Tweed tote

Luscious tweed yarn and chunky bobbles give this roomy tote bag a stylish look that will complement a cool outfit whatever the season. A cotton lining ensures the bag won't stretch, making this a very practical project, too.

YARN

Rowan *Scottish Tweed Chunky* (100% pure new wool), approx. 100g (3½oz)/100m (109yd) per ball

4 balls of Claret 013

NEEDLES

Set of four 7.00mm (US 10½) double-pointed needles

Pair of 7.00mm (US 10½) knitting needles

EXTRAS

Small amount of waste yarn (for cast on edge)

Stitch holder

Two 20-cm (8-in) diameter wooden rings (for handles)

Small amounts of silk or wool fibres (to fill bobbles) – optional

Piece of lining fabric 80cm (31½in) by 50cm (19½in)

Matching sewing thread

TENSION (GAUGE)

13½ sts and 19 rows = 10cm (4in) square measured over patt using 7.00mm (US 10½) needles

MEASUREMENTS

Completed bag is 36cm (14in) wide and 44cm (17¼in) tall.

SKILL LEVEL

Intermediate

BAG

Using 7.00mm (US 10½) needles and waste yarn, cast on 96 sts. Divide sts evenly across three dpns; join for working in the round.

Round 1: Knit.

Cut off waste yarn and join in main yarn, leaving a long end.

Now work in patt as follows:

Rounds 1–3: Knit.

Round 4: K2, *(k1, p1, k1) all into next st, k5; rep from * to last 4 sts, (k1, p1, k1) all into next st, k3.

Round 5: K2, *(k1, p1) into next st, k1, (p1, k1) into next st, k5; rep from * to last 6 sts, (k1, p1) into next st, k1, (p1, k1) into next st, k3.

Row 6: Knit.

Round 7: K2, *skpo, k1, k2tog, k5; rep from * to last 8 sts, skpo, k1, k2tog, k3.

Round 8: K2, *sl 1, k2tog, psso, k5; rep from * to last 6 sts, sl 1, k2tog, psso, k3 (96 sts).

Rounds 9–11: Knit.

Round 12: *K5, (k1, p1, k1) all into next st; rep from * to end.

Round 13: *K5, (k1, p1) into next st, k1, (p1, k1) into next st; rep from * to end.

Row 14: Knit.

Round 15: *K5, skpo, k1, k2tog; rep from * to end.

Round 16: *K5, sl 1, k2tog, psso; rep from * to end (96 sts).

Last 16 rounds form patt. (Note: number of sts varies while working patt. All st counts given presume each bobble – 1, 3 or 5 sts, depending on point in patt – counts as one st throughout.)

Work in patt for 40 rounds more, ending after patt round 8.

Round 57: [K5, skpo, k34, k2tog, k5] twice (92 sts).

Round 58: Knit.

DIVIDE FOR TOP SECTIONS

Slip last 46 sts of last round onto a holder for second top section. Slip first 46 sts of last round onto 7.00mm (US 10½) needles and now work in patt in rows on these sts as follows:

**Row 1 (RS): Sl 1, k4, skpo, k to last 7 sts, k2tog, k5 (44 sts).

Row 2: Sl 1, p9, *(p1, k1, p1) all into next st, p5; rep from * to last 10 sts, (p1, k1, p1) all into next st, p9.

Row 3: Sl 1, k4, skpo, k2, *(k1, p1) into next st, k1, (p1, k1) into next st, k5; rep from * 3 times more, (k1, p1) into next st, k1, (p1, k1) into next st, k3, k2tog, k5.

Row 4: Sl 1, purl to end.

Row 5: Sl 1, k4, skpo, k1, *skpo, k1, k2tog, k5; rep from * 3 times more, skpo, k1, k2tog, k2, k2tog, k5.

Row 6: Sl 1, p7, *p2tog and slip resulting st back onto LH needle, lift second st on LH needle over this st and off LH needle, then slip st back onto RH needle, p5; rep from * 3 times more, p2tog and slip resulting st back onto LH needle, lift second st on LH needle over this st and off LH needle, then slip st back onto RH needle, p7.

Row 7: As row 1 (38 sts).

Row 8: As row 4.

These 8 rows cont patt, but now worked in rows not rounds, and set decreases. Keeping patt correct and working all decreases as now set, cont as follows:

Dec 1 st at each end of next and foll 5 alt rows (26 sts).

Work 1 row.

Row 21: Sl 1, k4, skpo, k2, k2tog, *k5, skpo, k2tog; rep from * once more, k2tog, k5 (25 sts).

Work 1 row.

Row 23: Sl 1, k4, skpo, k to last 7 sts, k2tog, k5.

Row 24: Sl 1, purl to end.

Rep last 2 rows twice more (19 sts).

Row 29: Sl 1, knit to end.

Row 30: Sl 1, purl to end.

Rep last 2 rows twice more.

Cast (bind) off.

Return to sts left on holder, slip these sts onto 7.00mm (US 10½) needles and, working in patt in rows, complete as given for first top section from **.

FINISHING

Sew in all loose ends, block and press the pieces.

If desired, insert the silk or wool fibres inside each bobble of patt and secure in place with a few sewing sts on inside.

Lay Bag flat and cut out shape twice from lining fabric, adding seam allowance along all edges.

Using long end left at start of first round in main yarn and Kitchener stitch (see page 95), carefully graft sts of first round in main yarn together to form base seam, removing waste yarn at same time.

Make up lining to match knitted section.

Slip lining inside Bag, turn under raw edges around top sections and neatly sew in place.

Thread ends of top sections onto wooden rings, fold last 8 rows to inside and securely sew in place.

DESIGNED BY

Claire Garland

Cluster beach bag

Simple crochet stitches and vibrant stripes combine to make this modern bag that will hold all you need for a day by the sea.

YARN

Coats *Anchor Tapisserie Wool* (100% wool), approx. 10m (11yd) per skein

2 skeins of leaf green 9118 (A), 2 skeins of olive 9168 (B), 2 skeins of cobalt blue 8692 (C), 2 skeins of apple 9154 (D), 2 skeins of black 9800 (E), 2 skeins of bright red 8198 (F), 2 skeins of fuchsia pink 8486 (G), 2 skeins of sky 8684 (H), 5 skeins of bright orange 8194 (I), 2 skeins of yolk 8120 (J), 2 skeins of lime 9274 (K), 2 skeins of light blue 8672 (L), 2 skeins of lemon curd 8018 (M), 2 skeins of raspberry 8440 (N), 2 skeins of red plum 8424 (O), 7 skeins of bright gold 9284 (P), 2 skeins of lilac 8590 (Q), 2 skeins of jade 8966 (R), 2 skeins of orange ice lolly 8152 (S), 2 skeins of cream 8034 (T), 2 skeins of cyclamen 8456 (U), 2 skeins of grey 9790 (V), 2 skeins of cherry blossom 8484 (W), 2 skeins of turquoise 8936 (X)

NEEDLES

4.50mm (G/6) crochet hook

EXTRAS

Piece of lining fabric 60cm (23½in) by 70cm (27½in)
Piece of deep pink felt 30cm (12in) by 20cm (8in)
Piece of light pink felt 30cm (12in) by 20cm (8in)
Piece of red felt 70cm (27½in) by 12cm (4¾in)
Piece of card (for base) 18cm (7in) by 34cm (13½in)
Matching sewing thread
Purchased felt rose brooch – optional

TENSION (GAUGE)

7 clusters and 7 rows = 10cm (4in) square measured over patt using 4.50mm (G/6) hook

MEASUREMENTS

Completed bag is 34cm (131½in) wide, 23cm (9in) tall and 18cm (7in) deep (at base).

SKILL LEVEL

Intermediate

SPECIAL ABBREVIATIONS

See page 95 for information on cluster.

SIDES AND BASE

With A, make 51 ch.

Row 1: 1 dc (sc) into 2nd ch from hook, 1 dc (SC) into each ch to end, turn (50 sts).

Row 2: 1 ch (does NOT count as st), 1 dc (sc) into each dc (sc) to end, turn. Change to B.

Row 3: With B, 3 ch (counts as first st), miss dc (sc) at base of 3 ch, *1 cluster into next dc (sc), 1 ch, miss 1 dc (sc); rep from * to last 2 dc (sc), 1 ch, miss next dc (sc), 1 tr (dc) into last dc (sc), turn (24 clusters).

Joining in and breaking off colours as required, now work in patt as follows:

Row 4: With C, 3 ch, miss tr (dc) at base of 3 ch, 1 cluster into first ch sp, *1 ch, miss 1 cluster, 1 cluster into next ch sp; rep from * to last 2 sts, 1 ch, miss 1 cluster, 1 tr (dc) between first cluster and 3 ch at beg of previous row, turn. This row forms patt.

Keeping patt correct, now work in stripes as follows:

Row 5: With D.

Row 6: With E.

Row 7: With F.

Rows 8 and 9: With G.

Row 10: With H.

Row 11: With I.

Row 12: With J.

Row 13: With K.

Row 14: With L.

Row 15: With M.

Row 16: With N.

Row 17: With O.

Place markers at both ends of last row – this completes first side and marks bottom corners and beginning of base.

Rows 18–28: With P.

Place markers at both ends of last row – this completes base and marks bottom corners and beginning of second side.

Row 29: With B.

Row 30: With Q.

Row 31: With R.

Row 32: With S.

Row 33: With T.

Row 34: With I.

Row 35: With U.

Row 36: With H.

Row 37: With E.

Row 38: With V.

Row 39: With K.

Row 40: With W.

Rows 41 and 42: With X.

Row 43: With F.

Row 44: With I, 1 ch (does NOT count as st), 1 dc (sc) into tr (dc) at base of 1 ch, *1 dc (sc) into next ch sp, 1 dc (sc) into next cluster; rep from * to end, working dc (sc) at end of last rep into top of 3 ch at beg of previous row, turn.

Row 45: With I, 1 ch (does NOT count as st), 1 dc (sc) into each dc (sc) to end. Fasten off.

FIRST SIDE GUSSET

With O, make 29 ch.

Row 1: 1 dc (sc) into 2nd ch from hook, 1 dc (sc) into each ch to end, turn (28 sts).

Row 2: With O, 3 ch (counts as first st), miss dc (sc) at base of 3 ch, *1 cluster into next dc (sc), 1 ch, miss 1 dc (sc); rep from * to last 2 dc (sc), 1 ch, miss next dc (sc), 1 tr (dc) into last dc (sc), turn (13 clusters).

Joining in and breaking off colours as required, now work as follows:

Row 3: With N, 3 ch (counts as first st), miss (tr (dc) at base of 3 ch, 1 ch and first cluster), 1 cluster into next ch sp, *1 ch, miss 1 cluster, 1 cluster into next ch sp; rep from * to last 2 sts, 1 ch, miss 1 cluster, 1 tr (dc) between first cluster and 3 ch at beg of previous row, turn (12 clusters).

Row 4: As row 3 but with M (11 clusters).

Row 5: As row 3 but with I (10 clusters).

Row 6: As row 3 but with K (9 clusters).

Row 7: As row 3 but with J (8 clusters).

Row 8: As row 3 but with I (7 clusters).

Row 9: As row 3 but with H (6 clusters).

Rows 10 and 11: As row 3 but with G (4 clusters).

Row 12: With F, 3 ch, miss tr (dc) at base of 3 ch, 1 cluster into first ch sp, *1 ch, miss 1 cluster, 1 cluster into next ch sp; rep from * to last 2 sts, 1 ch, miss 1 cluster, 1 tr (dc) between first cluster and 3 ch at beg of previous row, turn. This row forms patt.

Keeping patt correct, cont as follows:

Row 13: With E.

Row 14: With D.

Row 15: With C.

Row 16: With B.

Row 17: With A, 1 ch (does NOT count as st), 1 dc (sc) into tr (dc) at base of 1 ch, *1 dc (sc) into next ch sp, 1 dc (sc) into next cluster; rep from * to end, working dc (sc) at end of last rep into top of 3 ch at beg of previous row, turn.

Row 18: With A, 1 ch (does NOT count as st), 1 dc (sc) into each dc (sc) to end. Fasten off.

SECOND SIDE GUSSET

With B, make 29 ch.

Row 1: 1 dc (sc) into 2nd ch from hook, 1 dc (sc) into each ch to end, turn (28 sts).

Complete as given for First Side Gusset, using colours as follows:

Row 2: With B.

Row 3: With Q.

Row 4: With R.

Row 5: With S.

Row 6: With T.
Row 7: With I.
Row 8: With U.
Row 9: With H.
Row 10: With E.
Row 11: With V.
Row 12: With K.
Row 13: With W.
Rows 14 and 15: With X.
Row 16: With F.
Rows 17 and 18: With I.
Fasten off.

FINISHING

Sew in all loose ends, block and press the pieces.

From lining fabric, cut out same size pieces as Sides and Base, and Gussets, adding seam allowance along all edges. Cut deep pink felt into four 30cm (12in) by 5cm (2in) strips. Enlarge the template below and pin a strip to it. Cut one edge of each strip to the scalloped shape. Run gathering threads along straight edge and pull up gathers to make edge approx. 20cm (8in) long.

Sew foundation ch edge of each Gusset to side of Base section between markers. Now sew row-end edges of Gussets and Sides together, enclosing gathered edge of scalloped felt strips in seams – match end of strips to markers so that other end of strip falls approx. 3cm (1in) below upper edge.

Trim red felt strip to 64cm (25in) long and join shorter ends to form a loop. Fold loop in half, then fold in raw edges, to create a loop approx. 5cm (2in) deep. Position this loop inside upper opening edge of bag, with 'open' folded edges at top, and neatly stitch in place around upper edge, leaving folds open.

Cut light pink felt into two 30cm (12in) by 10cm (4in) strips. Fold each strip in half lengthwise, then fold in raw edges, to create a strip approx. 2.5cm (1in) wide. Stitch along length to secure folds. Position each handle inside folded edges of red felt loop, positioning handles approx. 13cm (5in) apart as in photograph and sew in place by stitching through crochet sections, red felt loop and handles around entire upper opening edge.

Make up lining fabric in same way as crochet pieces. Turn under raw edges around upper opening edge. Slip card inside Bag and carefully attach to base section at corners. Slip lining inside Bag and slip stitch in place. If desired, attach rose brooch near base of one Handle.

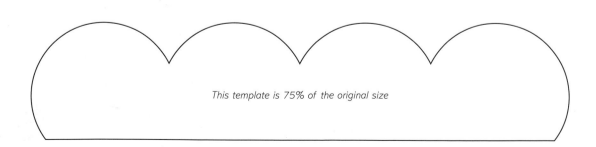

This template is 75% of the original size

DESIGNED BY

Sue Bradley

Duffle bag

This bag might look intricate, but it's just simple stripes worked in a double rib stitch, so all you need to do is knit and purl – easy! Team it with jeans for casual style or with a sundress for a summer beach look.

YARN

Rowan *Pure Wool Aran* (100% superwash wool), approx. 100g (3½oz)/170m (186yd) per ball

    1 ball of Ivory 670 (A)

    1 ball of Cedar 670 (B)

    1 ball of Paper 671 (C)

NEEDLES

Pair of 5.00mm (US 8) knitting needles

EXTRAS

Four 15-mm (⅝-in) diameter buttons

TENSION (GAUGE)

24 sts and 28 rows = 10cm (4in) square measured over patt using 5.00mm (US 8) needles

MEASUREMENTS

Completed bag is 40cm (15¾in) tall, with a base diameter of 20cm (8in).

SKILL LEVEL

Beginner

MAIN SECTION

With A, cast on 123 sts.

Row 1 (RS): K2, *p2, k2; rep from * to last st, p1.

Row 2: As row 1.

These 2 rows form stitch patt.

Work in patt for 2 rows more, ending with a WS row.

Keeping patt correct, now work in stripes as follows:

Row 5: With B.

Row 6: With C.

Rows 7 to 9: With A.

Last 5 rows form stripe sequence.

Cont in patt in stripe sequence as set for 8 rows more, ending with a RS row.

Next row (eyelet row) (WS): With A, k2, *p2tog, yon, k2; rep from * to end.

Cont in patt in stripe sequence as set until Main Section measures approx. 40cm (15¾in) from cast on edge, ending after 3 rows with A.

With A, work in patt for 1 row more.

Cast (bind) off.

BASE

With A, cast on 14 sts.

Starting with a knit row, work St st for 1 row, ending with a RS row.

Inc 1 st at each end of next 14 rows (40 sts).

Work 21 rows, ending with a WS row.

Dec 1 st at each end of next 14 rows, ending with a WS row.

Cast (bind) off rem 14 sts.

STRAPS (MAKE 2)

With A, cast on 8 sts.

Row 1: [K2, p2] twice.

Rep this row until Strap measures 50cm (19½in).

Cast (bind) off.

FINISHING

Sew in all loose ends. Do NOT press. Join row-end edges of Main Section to form a tube. Sew Base to cast (bound) off edge of Main Section, then fold along seam and stitch through both layers to accentuate base seam.

With B, make a twisted cord approx. 90cm (35½in) long and knot ends, leaving little tassels. Thread twisted cord through eyelet row and tie ends in a bow to close bag.

Using photograph as a guide, attach Straps near eyelet row and to base seam by securely sewing a button through end of Strap and Main Section.

TIP

Although each colour of yarn is used to make a single-row stripe or a three-row stripe, the stripe sequence has been designed so that the colour you need next will always be at the right end of a row when you need it. However, to keep the yarns to hand and prevent untidy loops forming along the edge of the knitting, you need to carry the yarns not in use up the side of the work. This is easy: when you get to the end of a row, swap to the new colour of yarn needed and before you start working the row, loop this yarn around the yarns not being used to hold them against the edge of the knitting. Do this at the end of every row and your edges will be tidy and the yarn you need next will always be just there, ready to go. Don't pull the yarns being carried too tight or you will tighten the edge of the knitting.

DESIGNED BY

Carol Meldrum

Chevron holdall

Waves of bold colour turn a simple shape into an attention-grabbing bag. Knitted in a cotton yarn that shows off stitch detail brilliantly, this bag will hold lots of kit whether you are on your way to work or out for the evening.

YARN

Rowan *Handknit Cotton* (100% cotton), approx. 50g (1¾oz)/85m (93yd) per ball

    2 balls of Decadent 314 (A)

    1 ball of Gooseberry 219 (B)

    1 ball of Thunder 335 (C)

    1 ball of Linen 205 (D)

    1 ball of Double Choc 315 (E)

NEEDLES

3.50mm (E/4) crochet hook

4.00mm (G/6) crochet hook

TENSION (GAUGE)

18 sts and 9 rows = 10cm (4in) square measured over tr (dc) fabric using 4.00mm (G/6) hook

MEASUREMENTS

Completed bag is 40cm (15¾in) wide (at base) and 29cm (11½in) tall.

SKILL LEVEL

Intermediate

SPECIAL ABBREVIATIONS

See page 95 for information on tr3tog (dc3tog), tr5tog (dc5tog).

SIDES (MAKE 2)

Using 3.50mm (E/4) hook and A, make 90 ch.

Row 1: 1 tr (dc) into 4th ch from hook, *1 tr (dc) into each of next 12 ch, tr3tog (dc3tog) over next 3 ch, 1 tr (dc) into each of next 12 ch**, 2 tr (dc) into each of next 2 ch; rep from * to end, ending last rep at **, 2 tr (dc) into last ch, turn (87 sts).

Row 2: 3 ch (counts as first tr (dc)), 1 tr (dc) into tr (dc) at base of 3 ch, *1 tr (dc) into each of next 12 tr (dc), tr3tog (dc3tog) over next 3 sts, 1 tr (dc) into each of next 12 tr (dc)**, 2 tr (dc) into each of next 2 tr (dc); rep from * to end, ending last rep at **, 2 tr (dc) into top of 3 ch at beg of prev row, turn.

Row 3: 3 ch (counts as first tr (dc)), 1 tr (dc) into tr (dc) at base of 3 ch, *1 tr (dc) into each of next 11 tr (dc), tr5tog (dc5tog) over next 5 sts, 1 tr (dc) into each of next 11 tr (dc)**, 2 tr (dc) into each of next 2 tr (dc); rep from * to end, ending last rep at **, 2 tr (dc) into top of 3 ch at beg of prev row, turn (81 sts).

Row 4: 3 ch (counts as first tr (dc)), 1 tr (dc) into tr (dc) at base of 3 ch, *1 tr (dc) into each of next 11 tr (dc), tr3tog (dc3tog) over next 3 sts, 1 tr (dc) into each of next 11 tr (dc)**, 2 tr (dc) into each of next 2 tr (dc); rep from * to end, ending last rep at **, 2 tr (dc) into top of 3 ch at beg of prev row, turn. Joining in and cutting off colours as required, now cont in stripes as follows:

Row 5: As row 4 but with B.

Row 6: With A, 3 ch (counts as first tr (dc)), 1 tr (dc) into tr (dc) at base of 3 ch, *1 tr (dc) into each of next 10 tr (dc), tr5tog (dc5tog) over next 5 sts, 1 tr (dc) into each of next 10 tr (dc)**, 2 tr (dc) into each of next 2 tr (dc); rep from * to end, ending last rep at **, 2 tr (dc) into top of 3 ch at beg of prev row, turn (75 sts).

Rows 7–8: With C, 3 ch (counts as first tr (dc)), 1 tr (dc) into tr (dc) at base of 3 ch, *1 tr (dc) into each of next 10 tr (dc), tr3tog (dc3tog) over next 3 sts, 1 tr (dc) into each of next 10 tr (dc)**, 2 tr (dc) into each of next 2 tr (dc); rep from * to end, ending last rep at **, 2 tr (dc) into top of 3 ch at beg of prev row, turn.

Row 9: With A, 3 ch (counts as first tr (dc)), 1 tr (dc) into tr (dc) at base of 3 ch, *1 tr (dc) into each of next 9 tr (dc), tr5tog (dc5tog) over next 5 sts, 1 tr (dc) into each of next 9 tr (dc)**, 2 tr (dc) into each of next 2 tr (dc); rep from * to end, ending last rep at **, 2 tr (dc) into top of 3 ch at beg of prev row, turn (69 sts).

Row 10: With D, 3 ch (counts as first tr (dc)), 1 tr (dc) into tr (dc) at base of 3 ch, *1 tr (dc) into each of next 9 tr (dc), tr3tog (dc3tog) over next 3 sts, 1 tr (dc) into each of next 9 tr (dc)**, 2 tr (dc) into each of next 2 tr (dc); rep from * to end, ending last rep at **, 2 tr (dc) into top of 3 ch at beg of prev row, turn.

Row 11: As row 10 but with B.

Row 12: With B, 3 ch (counts as first tr (dc)), 1 tr (dc) into tr (dc) at base of 3 ch, *1 tr (dc) into each of next 8 tr (dc), tr5tog (dc5tog) over next 5 sts, 1 tr (dc) into each of next 8 tr (dc)**, 2 tr (dc) into each of next 2 tr (dc); rep from * to end, ending last rep at **, 2 tr (dc) into top of 3 ch at beg of prev row, turn (63 sts).

Row 13: With C, 3 ch (counts as first tr (dc)), 1 tr (dc) into tr (dc) at base of 3 ch, *1 tr (dc) into each of next 8 tr (dc), tr3tog (dc3tog) over next 3 sts, 1 tr (dc) into each of next 8 tr (dc)**, 2 tr (dc) into each of next 2 tr (dc); rep from * to end, ending last rep at **, 2 tr (dc) into top of 3 ch at beg of prev row, turn.

Row 14: As row 13 but with A.

Row 15: With D, 3 ch (counts as first tr (dc)), 1 tr (dc) into tr (dc) at base of 3 ch, *1 tr (dc) into each of next 7 tr (dc), tr5tog (dc5tog) over next 5 sts, 1 tr (dc) into each of next 7 tr (dc)**, 2 tr (dc) into each of next 2 tr (dc); rep from * to end, ending last rep at **, 2 tr (dc) into top of 3 ch at beg of prev row, turn (57 sts).

Row 16: With D, 3 ch (counts as first tr (dc)), 1 tr (dc) into tr (dc) at base of 3 ch, *1 tr (dc) into each of next 7 tr (dc), tr3tog (dc3tog) over next 3 sts, 1 tr (dc) into each of next 7 tr (dc)**, 2 tr (dc) into each of next 2 tr (dc); rep from * to end, ending last rep at **, 2 tr (dc) into top of 3 ch at beg of prev row, turn.

Row 17: As row 16 but with B.

Row 18: With A, 3 ch (counts as first tr (dc)), 1 tr (dc) into tr (dc) at base of 3 ch, *1 tr (dc) into each of next 6 tr (dc), tr5tog (dc5tog) over next 5 sts, 1 tr (dc) into each of next 6 tr (dc)**, 2 tr (dc) into each of next 2 tr (dc); rep from * to end, ending last rep at **, 2 tr (dc) into top of 3 ch at beg of prev row, turn (51 sts).

Row 19: With C, 3 ch (counts as first tr (dc)), 1 tr (dc) into tr (dc) at base of 3 ch, *1 tr (dc) into each of next 6 tr (dc), tr3tog (dc3tog) over next 3 sts, 1 tr (dc) into each of next 6 tr (dc)**, 2 tr (dc) into each of next 2 tr (dc); rep from * to end, ending last rep at **, 2 tr (dc) into top of 3 ch at beg of prev row, turn.

Row 20: As row 19.

Row 21: With E, 1 ch (does NOT count as st), 1 dc (sc) into each of first 3 tr (dc), *1 htr (hdc) into each of next 3 tr (dc), 1 tr (dc) into each of next 5 sts, 1 htr (hdc) into each of next 3 tr (dc)**, 1 dc (sc) into each of next 6 tr (dc); rep from * to end, ending last rep at **, 1 dc (sc) into each of next 2 tr (dc), 1 dc (sc) into top of 3 ch at beg of prev row, turn.

Row 22: With E, 3 ch (counts as first tr (dc)), miss dc (sc) at base of 3 ch, 1 tr (dc) into each of next 7 sts, 1 ch, miss 1 st, 1 tr (dc) into each of next 33 sts, 1 ch, miss 1 st, 1 tr (dc) into each of last 8 sts, turn.

Row 23: With E, 3 ch (counts as first tr (dc)), miss tr (dc) at base of 3 ch, 1 tr (dc) into each tr (dc) and ch sp to end, working last tr (dc) into top of 3 ch at beg of prev row.
Fasten off.

HANDLE

Using 4.00mm (G/6) hook and two strands of E held together, make 151 ch.

Row 1: 1 ss (sl st) into 2nd ch from hook, 1 ss (sl st) into each ch to end.
Fasten off.

FINISHING

Sew in all loose ends, block and press the pieces.
Sew Sides together along row-end and foundation ch edges. Using photograph as a guide, thread Handle through 'holes' of row 22 and join ends of Handle securely.

DESIGNED BY

Fair Isle book bag

If you are new to Fair Isle knitting, this is a great project to start with. The sides are simple rectangles with no shaping, so you can concentrate on getting the colour patterning right without any other distractions.

YARN

Rowan *Scottish Tweed 4-ply* (100% pure new wool), approx. 25g (1oz)/110m (120yd) per ball

- 4 balls of Oatmeal 025 (A)
- 1 ball of Sea Green 006 (B)
- 1 ball of Porridge 024 (C)
- 1 ball of Peat 019 (D)
- 1 ball of Rust 009 (E)
- 1 ball of Gold 028 (F)

NEEDLES

Pair of 3.00mm (US 2) knitting needles

Pair of 3.25mm (US 3) knitting needles

EXTRAS

Piece of lining fabric 80cm (31½in) by 50cm (19½in)

Piece of card (for base) 35cm (14in) by 8cm (3in)

Matching sewing thread

TENSION (GAUGE)

28 sts and 38 rows = 10cm (4in) square measured over St st using 3.25mm (US 3) needles

MEASUREMENTS

Completed bag is 34cm (13½in) wide, 27cm (10½in) tall and 7cm (2¾in) deep.

SKILL LEVEL

Intermediate

SIDES (MAKE 2)

Using 3.25mm (US 3) needles and A,
cast on 72 sts.

Starting with a knit row, work in St st for
4 rows, ending with a WS row.

Repeating the 12-st patt rep 6 times
across each row, work the 22 chart rows
5 times, then chart rows 1 14 again.

Cut off all contrasts and cont using
A only.

Starting with a knit row, work in St st for
2 rows, ending with a WS row.

Cast (bind) off.

UPPER BORDERS (BOTH ALIKE)

Using 3.00mm (US 2) needles, with RS
facing and A, pick up and knit 130 sts
along one row-end edge of Side piece.

Row 1: *K1, p1; rep from * to end.
Row 2: *P1, k1; rep from * to end.

These 2 rows form moss (seed) st.

Work in moss (seed) st for 4 rows more,
ending with a RS row.

Cast (bind) off in moss (seed) st
(on WS).

GUSSET AND STRAP

Mark centre of lower row-end edge of
one Side piece.

Using 3.00mm (US 2) needles and A,
cast on 20 sts.

Work in moss (seed) st as given for
Upper Border until Gusset fits along

lower row-end edge of Side from centre marker to one corner.

Place markers at both ends of last row. Cont in moss (seed) st until Gusset, from markers, fits up side (cast on or cast (bound) off edge) of Side, to cast (bound) off edge of Upper Border.

Place markers at both ends of last row. First half of Gusset completed.

Cont in moss (seed) st until Strap, from last pair of markers, measures 70cm (27½in). Strap section completed.

Place markers at both ends of last row. Cont in moss (seed) st until Gusset, from last pair of markers, fits down other side (cast on or cast (bound) off edge) of Side to lower corner.

Place markers at both ends of last row. Cont in moss (seed) st until Gusset, from last pair of markers, fits along lower row-end edge of Side from corner to centre marker. Second half of Gusset completed.

Cast (bind) off.

FINISHING

Sew in all loose ends, block and press the pieces.

From lining fabric, cut out same size pieces as Sides and Upper Borders and gusset sections of Gusset and Strap, adding seam allowance along all edges. Join cast on and cast (bound) off ends of Gusset sections to form one long loop. Matching markers to corners of Sides and leaving Strap section free, sew Gusset sections to 3 edges of both Side pieces.

Trim card to fit neatly into base of Bag and slip inside Bag. Make up lining in same way as knitted pieces. Slip lining inside Bag, turn under raw edges around upper opening edge and neatly sew in place.

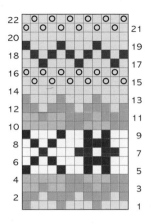

Key

▢	Oatmeal 025 (A)
⊙	Oatmeal 025 (A) P on RS, K on WS
▨	Sea Green 006 (B)
☐	Porridge 024 (C)
■	Peat 019 (D)
■	Rust 009 (E)
▨	Gold 028 (F)

TIP

If you are worried that the bag handle might stretch under the weight of the books you'll carry, sew a length of grosgrain ribbon to the back of it, sewing the ribbon to the lining at each end.

DESIGNED BY

Precious silk bag

Made in hot pink silk and an open lace knit pattern, this little bag has serious style.
For added colour, the contrast lining fabric shows through the lace – and stops your
possessions tumbling to the floor.

YARN

Debbie Bliss *Pure Silk* (100% pure silk), approx. 50g
(1¾oz)/125m (136yd) per skein
  1 skein of Rose 27012

NEEDLES

Set of four 5.00mm (US 8) double-pointed needles (dpns)
Pair of 5.00mm (US 8) knitting needles

EXTRAS

Small amount of waste yarn (for cast on edge)
Stitch holder
110cm (43½in) of fairly thick wire (for handles)
Selection of beads and charms (bag in photograph features
African copper beads, Shiana and Tibetan silver beads, black
and white silver charms and antique heishi beads)
Piece of lining fabric 35cm (13¾in) by 20cm (8in)
Matching sewing thread

TENSION (GAUGE)

30 sts and 19 rows = 10cm (4in) square measured over patt
using 5.00mm (US 8) needles

MEASUREMENTS

Completed bag is 12cm (4¾in) wide and 14cm (5½in) tall
(excluding handles).

SKILL LEVEL

Intermediate

BAG

Using 5.00mm (US 8) needles and waste yarn, cast on 72 sts. Divide sts evenly across three dpns; join for working in the round.

Round 1: Knit.

Cut off waste yarn and join in main yarn, leaving a long end.

Now work in patt as follows:

Round 1: Purl.

Round 2: Knit to end, winding yarn round needle 3 times for each st.

Round 3: Purl to end, dropping extra loops.

Round 4: *K5tog, (p1, k1, p1, k1, p1) all into next st; rep from * to end.

Round 5: Purl.

Round 6: *(P1, k1, p1, k1, p1) all into next st, k5tog; rep from * to end.

These 6 rounds form patt.

Work in patt for 13 rounds more, ending after patt round 1, turn.

DIVIDE FOR TOP SECTIONS

Slip first 36 sts of last round onto a holder for second top section. Slip last 36 sts of last round onto 5.00mm (US 8) needles and now work in rows on these sts as follows:

Row 1 (WS): *(K1, p1, k1, p1, k1) all into next st, p5tog; rep from * to end.

Row 2: Purl.

Row 3: *P5tog, (k1, p1, k1, p1, k1) all into next st; rep from * to end.

Row 4: Purl.

Rows 5–6: As rows 1 and 2.

Row 7: Purl.

Row 8: Knit.

Rows 9–10: As rows 7 and 8.

Cast (bind) off.

Return to sts left on holder, slip these sts onto 5.00mm (US 8) needles and, working in rows, complete as given for first top section from **.

FINISHING

Sew in all loose ends. Do NOT press. Lay Bag flat and cut out shape twice from lining fabric, adding seam allowance along all edges.

Using long end left at start of first round in main yarn and Kitchener stitch (see page 95), carefully graft sts of first round in main yarn together to form base seam, removing waste yarn at same time.

Make up lining to match knitted section. Slip lining inside Bag, turn under raw edges around top sections and neatly sew in place. Fold approx. 2cm (¾in) to inside across top of top sections and sew in place, forming channels to support bars for handles.

To form handles, cut two 33cm (13in) lengths of wire. Carefully bend wire into a U shape, with ends approx. 13cm (5in) apart. Form one end into a small loop. Thread beads and/or charms onto wire and then form free end into a matching small loop.

To make the bars that hold the Bag to the handles, cut two 21cm (8¼in) pieces of wire. Thread these lengths of wire through the channels across the top of the Bag and then through the loops at the ends of the handles. Form each end of these wires into small loops to secure everything in place.

TIP

Choice of lining fabric is important for this project as the lining shows through the knitting. A lovely silk in a toning or contrast colour is ideal. If you zigzag stitch and then trim the raw edges after making up the lining, it won't fray too much.

DESIGNED BY

Carol Meldrum

Uber bag

Combining the fashion for huge bags with the hot craft of crochet, this capacious tote is perfectly on trend. A variegated yarn creates intricate colour patterning with no effort and is set off by the rich chocolate handles.

YARN

Designer Yarns *Araucania Pomaire* (100% pima cotton), approx. 100g (3½oz)/168m (183yd) per ball

  3 balls of multi 01 (A)

Rowan *Handknit Cotton* (100% cotton), approx. 50g (1¾oz)/85m (93yd) per ball

  2 balls of Double Choc 315 (B)

NEEDLES

3.00mm (D/3) crochet hook

5.00mm (H/8) crochet hook

EXTRAS

Four stud fasteners

TENSION (GAUGE)

16½ sts = 10cm (4in) and 6 rows = 12.5cm (5in) measured over patt using 5.00mm (H/8) hook

MEASUREMENTS

Completed bag is 48cm (19in) wide and 40cm (15¾in) tall (excluding handles).

SKILL LEVEL

Advanced

SPECIAL ABBREVIATIONS

See page 95 for information on qtr (tr tr).

RIGHT SIDE PANELS (MAKE 2)

Using 5.00mm (H/8) hook and A, make 41 ch.

Row 1 (WS): 1 dc (sc) into 2nd ch from hook, 1 dc (sc) into each ch to end, turn (40 sts).

Now work in patt as follows:

Row 2: 6 ch, insert hook into 2nd ch from hook, yoh and draw loop through, [insert hook into next ch, yoh and draw loop through] 4 times, insert hook into dc (sc) at base of 6 ch, yoh and draw loop through (7 loops on hook), [yoh and draw through 2 loops] 6 times – this forms first linked qtr (tr tr), working down side of st just made: insert hook through first loop along side of st, yoh and draw loop through, [insert hook into next loop along side of st, yoh and draw loop through] 4 times, insert hook into next dc (sc), yoh and draw loop through (7 loops on hook), [yoh and draw through 2 loops] 6 times – this forms 1 linked qtr (tr tr), 1 linked qtr (tr tr) into each dc (sc) to end, turn.

Row 3: 1 ch (does NOT count as st), 1 dc (sc) into each st to end, turn.

Last 2 rows form patt.

Work in patt for 12 rows more.

SHAPE UPPER EDGE

Row 16: 6 ch, work first 22 linked qtr (tr tr), **working down side of st just made: miss first loop along side of st,

[insert hook into next loop along side of st, yoh and draw loop through] 4 times, insert hook into next dc (sc), yoh and draw loop through (6 loops on hook), [yoh and draw through 2 loops] 5 times, working down side of st just made: miss first loop along side of st, [insert hook into next loop along side of st, yoh and draw loop through] 3 times, insert hook into next dc (sc), yoh and draw loop through (5 loops on hook), [yoh and draw through 2 loops] 4 times, working down side of st just made: miss first loop along side of st, [insert hook into next loop along side of st, yoh and draw loop through] twice, insert hook into next dc (sc), yoh and draw loop through (4 loops on hook), [yoh and draw through 2 loops] 3 times, working down side of st just made: miss first loop along side of st just made: miss first loop along side of st, insert hook into next loop along side of st, yoh and draw loop through, insert hook into next dc (sc), yoh and draw loop through (3 loops on hook), [yoh and draw through 2 loops] twice, 1 dc (sc) into next dc (sc), 1 ss (sl st) into next dc (sc)**, turn.

Row 17: Miss ss (sl st) at end of prev row, 1 ss (sl st) into each of next 6 sts, 1 ch (does NOT count as st), 1 dc (sc) into st at base of 1 ch (this is last linked qtr (tr tr) of prev row), 1 dc (sc) into each st to end, turn.

Row 18: 6 ch, work first 16 linked qtr (tr tr), rep from ** to ** as given for row 16, turn.

Row 19: As row 17 (16 sts).
Work in patt on these 16 sts for 2 rows more.
Fasten off.

LEFT SIDE PANELS (MAKE 2)

Work as given for Right Side Panel to start of upper edge shaping.

SHAPE UPPER EDGE

Row 16: ss (sl st) across and into 13th st, 1 dc (sc) into next st, **1 ch, insert hook into side of dc (sc) just worked, yoh and draw loop through, insert hook into next dc (sc), yoh and draw loop through (3 loops on hook), [yoh and draw through 2 loops] twice, 1 ch, working down side of st just made: insert hook into first loop along side of st, yoh and draw loop through, insert hook into next loop along side of st, yoh and draw loop through, insert hook into next dc (sc), yoh and draw loop through (4 loops on hook), [yoh and draw through 2 loops] 3 times, 1 ch, working down side of st just made: insert hook into first loop along side of st, yoh and draw loop through, [insert hook into next loop along side of st, yoh and draw loop through] twice, insert hook into next dc (sc), yoh and draw loop through (5 loops on hook), [yoh and draw through 2 loops] 4 times, 1 ch, working down side of st just made: insert hook into first loop along side of st, yoh and draw loop through, [insert hook into next loop along side of st, yoh and draw loop through] 3 times, insert hook into next dc (sc), yoh and draw loop through (6 loops on hook), [yoh and draw through 2 loops] 5 times, 1 ch, working down side of st just made: insert hook into first loop along side of st, yoh and draw loop through, [insert hook into next loop along side of st, yoh and draw loop through] 4 times, insert hook into next dc (sc), yoh and draw loop through (7 loops on hook), [yoh and draw through 2 loops] 6 times – this forms first complete linked qtr (tr tr)**, 1 linked qtr (tr tr) into each dc (sc) to end, turn.

Row 17: 1 ch (does NOT count as st), 1 dc (sc) into each of first 22 sts, turn.

Row 18: 1 ch (does NOT count as st), miss first dc (sc), 1 dc (sc) into next dc (sc), rep from ** to ** as given for row 16, 1 linked qtr (tr tr) into each dc (sc) to end, turn.

Row 19: 1 ch (does NOT count as st), 1 dc (sc) into each of first 16 sts, turn. (16 sts).
Work in patt on these 16 sts for 2 rows more.
Fasten off.

HANDLES (MAKE 2)

Using 3.00mm (D/3) hook and B, make 150 ch and, taking care not to twist ch, join with a ss (sl st) to form a ring.

Round 1: 1 ch (does NOT count as st), 1 dc (sc) into each ch to end, ss (sl st) to first dc (sc), turn (150 sts).

Round 2: 3 ch (counts as first tr (dc)), miss first dc (sc), 1 tr (dc) into each of next 8 dc (sc), 2 tr (dc) into next dc (sc), *1 tr (dc) into each of next 9 dc (sc), 2 tr (dc) into next dc (sc); rep from * to end, ss (sl st) to top of 3 ch at beg of round, turn (165 sts).

Round 3: 3 ch (counts as first tr (dc)), miss first dc (sc), 1 tr (dc) into each of next 9 tr (dc), 2 tr (dc) into next tr (dc), *1 tr (dc) into each of next 10 tr (dc), 2 tr (dc) into next tr (dc); rep from * to end, ss (sl st) to top of 3 ch at beg of round, turn (180 sts).

Round 4: 1 ch (does NOT count as st), 1 dc (sc) into each tr (dc) to end, ss (sl st) to first dc (sc).

Fasten off.

FINISHING

Sew in all loose ends, block and press the pieces.

Joining pieces with WS together (so seam forms a ridge on RS), sew one Right Side Panel to one Left Side Panel along shorter row-end edges, forming a rectangle with a U shape cut out at top. Lay one Handle onto these pieces so that Handle fits the U shape and sew in place along U-shaped edge, following the photograph.

Join other Side Panels and Handle in the same way. Now sew Side Panels together along longer row-end and foundation ch edges.

At top 'corners' of Side Panels, fold edges in to form a pleat as in photograph. Attach a press fastener to hold pleat in place.

To hold Handles together, attach press fasteners approx. 10cm (4in) above upper opening edge of Sides

> ### TIP
>
> You can line the bag with study cotton if you want; this will help prevent the crochet fabric stretching if you overload your giant tote. Cut pieces of cotton fabric the same size as the Side Panels and make them up in the same way as the crochet pieces. Slip lining inside Bag, turn under raw edges around top and neatly sew in place.

DESIGNED BY

Sue Bradley

Lace evening purse

A simple repeat lace pattern is given a new twist by working it in a variegated colour yarn. The changing tones of cream give a vintage feel and make the lace stitches look more complex than they really are.

YARN

Rowan *Damask* (57% viscose, 22% linen, 21% acrylic), approx. 50g (1¾oz)/105m (115yd) per ball

  2 balls of Mica 040

NEEDLES

Pair of 3.75mm (US 5) knitting needles

EXTRAS

2m (2¼yd) of 6-mm (¼-in) thick shiny cord

Piece of lining fabric 80cm (31½in) by 30cm (11¾in)

Matching sewing thread

TENSION (GAUGE)

24 sts and 29 rows = 10cm (4in) square measured over patt using 3.75mm (US 5) needles

MEASUREMENTS

Completed bag is 24cm (9½in) tall, with a base diameter of 14cm (5½in).

MAIN SECTION

Cast on 121 sts.

Row 1 (RS): P2, *k5, p2; rep from * to end.

Row 2: K2, *p5, k2; rep from * to end.

Row 3: P2, *k2tog, yfwd, k1, yfwd, skpo, p2; rep from * to end.

Row 4: As row 2.

These 4 rows form patt.

Cont in patt until Main Section measures 24cm (9½in) from cast on edge, ending with a WS row.

Cast (bind) off.

BASE

Cast on 7 sts.

Starting with a knit row, work St st as follows:

Work 1 row.

Cast on 3 sts at beg of next 4 rows, then 2 sts at beg of foll 4 rows (27 sts).

Inc 1 st at beg of next 3 rows (30 sts).

Work 2 rows.

Inc 1 st at beg of next 2 rows (32 sts).

Work 6 rows.

Dec 1 st at beg of next 2 rows (30 sts).

Work 2 rows.

Dec 1 st at beg of next 3 rows (27 sts).

Cast (bind) off 2 sts at beg of next 4 rows, then 3 sts at beg of foll 4 rows.

Cast (bind) off rem 7 sts.

FINISHING

Sew in all loose ends, block and press knitted pieces.

From lining fabric, cut out same size pieces as Main Section and Base, adding seam allowance along all edges. Join row-end edges of Main Section to form a tube. Sew Base to cast (bound) off edge of Main Section.

Make up lining in same way. Slip lining inside Bag, turn under raw edge around upper edge and neatly sew in place. Cut a 70cm (27½in) length of cord and tie a knot in each end approx. 9cm (3½in) from cut ends. Unravel cut ends to form tassels. Thread this length of cord through eyelet holes of 5th patt repeat from upper edge, pull up to gather top of Bag and tie ends together loosely.

Thread remaining length of cord (this length forms handle) through eyelet rows of 4th patt repeat from upper edge at opposite side of Bag to where ends of previous length are. Knot both ends of this length of cord together approx. 12cm (4¾in) from end and unravel cut ends of cord to form a tassel.

TIP

You only need a small amount of fabric for the lining and it won't take much strain, so splash out on something luxurious, like satin or soft silk. These fabrics do fray, so neaten the edges with zigzag stitch and trim excess seam allowances after making up the lining section.

DESIGNED BY

Carol Meldrum

Denim satchel

Crisp cream denim yarn and simple crochet stitches make for a contemporary take on the classic satchel. An outer pocket closed with a strap adds practical storage as well as decorative detailing.

YARN

Rowan *Denim* (100% cotton), approx. 50g (1¾oz)/93m (101yd) per ball

  5 balls of Ecru 324

NEEDLES

4.00mm (G/6) crochet hook

EXTRAS

20cm (8in) zip

Two 4cm (1½in) by 1.5cm (⅝in) rectangular metal rings

Piece of card (for base) 23cm (9in) by 7cm (2¾in)

TENSION (GAUGE)

After washing: 15 sts and 9 rows = 10cm (4in) square measured over tr (dc) fabric using 4.00mm (G/6) hook

Note: Rowan Denim will shrink when washed for first time. All measurements given relate to measurements after washing.

MEASUREMENTS

Completed bag is 23cm (9in) wide, 28cm (11in) tall and 7cm (2¾in) deep.

SKILL LEVEL

Intermediate

SIDES (MAKE 2)

Make 37 ch.

Row 1: 1 tr (dc) into 4th ch from hook, 1 tr (dc) into each ch to end, turn (35 sts).

Row 2: 3 ch (counts as first tr (dc)), miss tr (dc) at base of 3 ch, 1 tr (dc) into each tr (dc) to end, working last tr (dc) into top of 3 ch at beg of prev row, turn. Last row forms tr (dc) fabric.

Work in tr (dc) fabric for 23 rows more.

SHAPE TOP GUSSET SECTION

Row 26: ss (sl st) along side of last tr (dc) of prev row and down almost to base of this tr (dc), 3 ch (counts as first tr (dc)), miss tr (dc) at base of 3 ch, 1 tr (dc) around stem of next and every tr (dc) to end, working last tr (dc) around stem of 3 ch at beg of prev row, turn. (Ridge created by this row forms fold line across top of Bag.)

Row 27: 1 ch (does NOT count as st), 1 dc (sc) into each st to end, working last dc (sc) into top of 3 ch at beg of prev row.

Fasten off.

GUSSET

Make 13 ch.

Row 1: 1 tr (dc) into 4th ch from hook, 1 tr (dc) into each ch to end, turn (11 sts).

Work in tr (dc) fabric as given for Sides for 69 rows.
Fasten off.

POCKET

Make 23 ch.
Row 1: 1 tr (dc) into 4th ch from hook, 1 tr (dc) into each ch to end, turn (21 sts).
Work in tr (dc) fabric as given for Sides for 9 rows.
Fasten off.

POCKET FLAP

Make 23 ch.
Row 1: 1 tr (dc) into 4th ch from hook, 1 tr (dc) into each ch to end, turn (21 sts).
Work in tr (dc) fabric as given for Sides for 7 rows.
Fasten off.

POCKET STRAP

Make 28 ch.
Row 1: 1 tr (dc) into 4th ch from hook, 1 tr (dc) into each ch to end, turn (26 sts).
Work in tr (dc) fabric as given for Sides for 2 rows.
Fasten off.

POCKET TAB

Make 23 ch.
Row 1: 1 tr (dc) into 4th ch from hook, 1 tr (dc) into each ch to end (11 sts).
Fasten off.

STRAP

Make 143 ch.
Row 1: 1 tr (dc) into 4th ch from hook, 1 tr (dc) into each ch to end, turn (141 sts).
Work in tr (dc) fabric as given for Sides for 2 rows.
Fasten off.

FINISHING

Sew in all loose ends. Do NOT press. Machine hot-wash all pieces (and small ball of yarn for seaming) following ball band instructions to shrink them to correct size. Once dry, block and press the pieces.
Using photograph as a guide, sew Pocket centrally onto one Side piece – position lower edge of Pocket 5 rows up from foundation ch edge. Sew Pocket Strap onto Pocket Flap as in photograph – one end of Strap will extend beyond lower edge of Flap. Sew Flap to Side above Pocket. Sew Pocket Tab onto Pocket to correspond with end of Strap.

Insert zip between upper (last row) edges of Sides.
Mark centre point of row-end edges of Gusset. With WS together (so seams form a ridge on RS) and matching this centre point to centre point of foundation ch edge of Sides, sew Gusset to foundation ch and row-end edges of Sides, stopping level with ridge row – Gusset should extend beyond ridge row for approx. 2 rows. Thread metal rings onto these extensions, fold over ends of Gusset and securely sew in place, attaching row-end edges of top gusset sections at same time.
Thread ends of Strap onto rings, fold under 4cm (1½in) and sew securely in place.
At base of Bag, fold gusset level with corners and sew across Gusset to form a ridge (to match other seams). Slip card inside Bag and secure to base section.

DESIGNED BY

Jacobean tote

Exotic flowers in jewel colours and clever handle detailing make this bag into something special. The main panels have no shaping, so there is just the colour knitting to concentrate on.

YARN

Rowan *Pure Wool DK* (100% superwash wool), approx. 50g (1¾oz)/125m (136yd) per ball

4 balls of Hay 014 (A)

Small amounts of same yarn in the following colours for intarsia pattern:

Pomegranate 029 (B), Gilt 032 (C), Hessian 016 (D), Cypress 007 (E), Indigo 010 (F), Damson 030 (G), Parsley 020 (H), Shamrock 023 (I) and Spice 034 (J)

NEEDLES

Pair of 3.25mm (US 3) knitting needles
Pair of 4.00mm (US 6) knitting needles

TENSION (GAUGE)

22 sts and 30 rows = 10cm (4in) square measured over St st using 4.00mm (US 6) needles

MEASUREMENTS

Completed bag is 41cm (16in) wide and 33cm (13in) tall.

SKILL LEVEL

Advanced

SIDES (MAKE 2)

Using 4.00mm (US 6) needles and A, cast on 90 sts.

Starting with a knit row, work in St st from chart until all 90 rows of chart have been completed, ending with a WS row. Cut off contrasts and cont with A only. Change to 3.25mm (US 3) needles. Work in garter st for 22 rows, ending with a WS row.

Cast (bind) off.

BASE

Using 4.00mm (US 6) needles and A, cast on 70 sts.

Starting with a knit row, work in St st as follows:

Work 1 row, ending with a RS row.

Cast on 3 sts at beg of next 6 rows (88 sts).

Work 6 rows, ending with a RS row.

Cast (bind) off 3 sts at beg of next 6 rows, ending with a RS row.

Cast (bind) off rem 70 sts.

HANDLES (MAKE 2)

Using 3.25mm (US 3) needles and A, cast on 11 sts.

Row 1 (RS): Knit.

Row 2: K1, p9, k1.

Rep these 2 rows until Handle measures 116cm (45½in), ending with a WS row.

Cast (bind) off.

HANDLE LOOPS (MAKE 4)

Using 3.25mm (US 3) needles and A, cast on 11 sts.

Row 1 (RS): Knit.

Row 2: K1, p9, k1.

Rep these 2 rows until Handle Loop measures 10cm (4in), ending with a WS row.

Cast (bind) off.

FINISHING

Embroider stem-stitch curls onto Sides as shown on chart.

Sew in all loose ends, block and press. Join sides along row-end edges. Sew Base to cast on edges of Sides, matching side seams to centre of Base row-end edges. Around upper opening edge, fold garter st section in half to inside and slip stitch in place.

Join row-end edges of Handle Loops, to form four short tubes. Using photograph as a guide, sew ends of Handle Loops inside upper edge of Bag, positioning Loops approx. 4cm (1½in) in from side seams.

Join row-end edges of Handles, to form two long tubes. Starting on RS of work, take one end of one Handle through one Handle Loop on one side, then take other end of same Handle through other Handle Loop of same Side. Join ends of Handle. Thread ends of other Handle through Handle Loops of other Side and join ends in same way.

Key

☐ Hay 014 (A)
■ Pomegranate 029 (B)
☐ Gilt 032 (C)
■ Hessian 016 (D)
■ Cypress 007 (E)
■ Indigo 010 (F)
■ Damson 030 (G)
■ Parsley 020 (H)
■ Shamrock 023 (I)
■ Spice 034 (J)

TIP

The flower shapes should be worked using the intarsia technique, but the detailing within them is best done using the Fair Isle technique. For intarsia instructions, turn to page 89 and for Fair Isle, turn to page 90. You can work the flower pattern on one side of the bag only and just knit the other side in plain cream if you prefer. You may need an extra ball of the cream yarn to do this.

DESIGNED BY

Claire Garland

Tweedy shopper

A capacious shopping bag that will happily swallow all sorts of goodies, whether you are shopping for salad or shoes. The pretty crochet frill and flower are simple to make, so are perfect for beginners to crochet.

YARN

Debbie Bliss *Donegal Chunky Tweed* (100% wool), approx. 100g (3½oz)/100m (109yd) per skein

　2 skeins of Peacock 09 (A)

GGH *Bel Air* (90% merino wool, 10% nylon), approx. 50g (1¾oz)/130m (142yd) per ball

　1 ball of Mauve 02 (B)

Coats *Anchor Tapisserie Wool* (100% wool), approx. 10m (11yd) per skein

　1 skein of lime 9274 (C)

NEEDLES

Pair of 9.00mm (US 13) knitting needles
6.00mm (J/10) crochet hook

EXTRAS

Four 25-mm (1-in) diameter red buttons
Stitch holder
Piece of card (for base) 36cm (14in) by 8cm (3in)

TENSION (GAUGE)

10 sts and 15 rows = 10cm (4in) square measured over St st using A and 9.00mm (US 13) needles.

MEASUREMENTS

Completed bag is 36cm (14in) wide, 42cm (16½in) tall and 8cm (3in) deep.

SKILL LEVEL

Beginner

SPECIAL ABBREVIATIONS

See page 95 for information on tr3tog (dc3tog).

SIDES AND BASE

Using 9.00mm (US 13) needles and A,
cast on 36 sts.

Starting with a purl row, work in
Rev st st for 38cm (15in), ending with
a WS row.

Place markers at both ends of last row
– these denote start of base section.

Starting with a knit row, work in St st
until work measures 8cm (3in) from
markers, ending with a WS row.

Place markers at both ends of last row
– these denote end of base section.

Starting with a purl row, work in
Rev st st until work measures 38cm
(15in) from second set of markers,
ending with a WS row.

Cast (bind) off.

GUSSETS (BOTH ALIKE)

Using 9.00mm (US 13) needles, with
WS facing (so that 'seam' shows on RS)
and A, pick up and knit 12 sts along
row-end edge of Sides and Base
between markers denoting base.

Starting with a purl row, work in
Rev st st until Gusset measures 32cm
(12½in) from pick-up row, ending with a
WS row.

DIVIDE FOR SIDE OPENINGS

Next row (RS): P6 and turn, leaving
rem 6 sts on a holder.

Cont in Rev st st on this set of 6 sts only until Gusset measures 38cm (15in) from pick-up row, ending with a WS row. Cast (bind) off.

Return to sts left on holder, rejoin A with RS facing and Pp to end.

Cont in Rev st st on this set of 6 sts only until Gusset measures 38cm (15in) from pick-up row, ending with a WS row. Cast (bind) off.

CROCHET EDGING

Sew row-end edges of Gussets to corresponding row-end edges of Sides, matching cast (bound) off edges of Gussets to cast on (or cast (bound) off) edges of Sides – sew seams with WS together so that seams show on RS. Using 6.00mm (J/10) crochet hook, with RS facing and B, attach yarn at base of one Gusset opening and work one round of dc (sc) evenly around entire upper opening edge, ensuring number of dc (sc) worked is divisible by 4 and ending with ss (sl st) to first dc (sc).

Next round: 1 ch (does NOT count as st), 1 dc (sc) into each dc (sc) to end, ss (sl st) to first dc (sc).

Rep last round once more.

Next round: 1 ch (does NOT count as st), 1 dc (sc) into first dc (sc), *miss 1 dc (sc), 5 tr (dc) into next dc (sc), miss 1 dc

(sc), 1 dc (sc) into next dc (sc); rep from * to end, replacing dc (sc) at end of last rep with ss (sl st) to first dc (sc). Fasten off.

HANDLES (MAKE 2)

Using 9.00mm (US 13) needles and A, cast on 6 sts.

Starting with a knit row, work 37 rows in St st, ending with a RS row.

Cast (bind) off.

FLOWER

Using 6.00mm (J/10) crochet hook and C, make 4 ch and join with a ss (sl st) to form a ring.

Round 1: 1 ch (does NOT count as st), 8 dc (sc) into ring, ss (sl st) to first dc (sc) (8 sts).

Round 2: 3 ch, tr3tog (dc3tog) into first dc (sc), *3 ch, 1 dc (sc) into centre ring**, 3 ch, miss next dc (sc) of round 1, tr3tog (dc3tog) into next dc (sc); rep from * to end, ending last rep at **, 1 ss (sl st) into first of 3 ch at beg of round, 6 ch, 1 ss (sl st) into 2nd ch from hook, 1 ss (sl st) into each of next 4 ch (to form stem).

Fasten off.

FINISHING

Sew in all loose ends, block and press the pieces.

Run gathering threads (with A) across top of Gussets just below opening and pull up to gather top of Gusset to 5cm (2in) wide. Fasten off securely.

Using photograph as a guide, sew Handles to top of Sides, positioning ends of Handles approx. 14cm (5½in) apart. Attach buttons to ends of Handles as in photograph. With A, attach Flower near end of one Handle by working several straight stitches radiating out from centre of Flower. Trim card to fit base of Bag and slip inside Bag and secure in place.

TIP

If you are a keen shopper and like to fill your shopping bag, you can line it to make it stronger. Before sewing the gussets to the sides, lay the Bag flat on a piece of heavy cotton fabric and draw around it, adding seam allowance along all edges. Make up the lining in the same way as the Bag. After finishing the Bag, slip the lining into it. Turn under raw edges around upper edge and neatly slip stitch in place. You can also stitch lengths of grosgrain ribbon to the backs of the handles to stop them stretching.

Fair Isle carpet bag

This bag is the ideal travelling companion; it's good-looking, will hold cabin essentials on a flight and see you through both daytime meetings and evening parties. What more could a girl want!

YARN

Rowan *Big Wool* (100% merino wool), approx. 100g (3½oz)/80m (87yd) per ball

- 2 balls of White Hot 001 (A)
- 1 ball of Linen 048 (B)
- 1 ball of Whoosh 014 (C)
- 1 ball of Glamour 036 (D)
- 1 ball of Bohemian 028 (E)
- 1 ball of Wild Berry 025 (F)

Coats *Anchor Tapisserie Wool* (100% wool), approx. 10m (11yd) per skein

- 2 skeins of red 8202 (G)

NEEDLES

Pair of 15.00mm (US 19) knitting needles
Pair of 4.00mm (US 6) knitting needles

EXTRAS

Stitch holder

Four 38-mm (1½-in) diameter self cover buttons

Piece of lining fabric 50cm (19½in) by 79cm (31in)

Matching sewing thread

Decorative crystal brooch (optional)

TENSION (GAUGE)

7 sts and 10½ rows = 10cm (4in) square measured over St st using Rowan Big Wool and 15.00mm (US 19) needles

MEASUREMENTS

Completed bag is 39cm (15½in) wide, 29cm (11½in) tall and 16cm (6¼in) deep.

SKILL LEVEL

Intermediate

SIDES (MAKE 2)

Using 15.00mm (US 19) needles and A, cast on 37 sts.

Row 1(RS): Knit.

Row 2: Purl.

Starting with a knit row, work 21 rows in St st from chart A, ending with a RS row.

Row 24: With A, purl.

Row 25: With A, knit.

Cast (bind) off.

GUSSET

Using 15.00mm (US 19) needles and B, cast on 12 sts.

Starting with a knit row, work 25 rows in St st, ending with a RS row. (This section fits down first row-end edge of Sides.)

Place markers at both ends of last row – these match to first lower corners of Sides.

Cont in garter st until Gusset, from markers, fits across cast-on edge of Side section, ending with a WS row.

Place markers at both ends of last row – these match to second lower corners of Sides.

Starting with a knit row, work 25 rows in St st, ending with a RS row. (This section fits up other row-end edge of Sides.)

Next row (WS): Knit (to form fold line). Place markers at both ends of last row – these match to first top corners of Sides.

Work in St st for 5 rows more, ending with a WS row.

SHAPE OPENING

Next row (RS): With C, k6 and turn, leaving rem 6 sts on a holder.

Work in St st with C for 28 rows more, ending with a RS row.

Change to B.

Starting with a purl row, work in St st with B for 5 rows.

Cast (bind) off.

Return to sts left on holder and rejoin C with RS facing.

Starting with a knit row, work in St st with C for 29 rows, ending with a RS row.

Change to B.

Starting with a purl row, work in St st with B for 5 rows.

Cast (bind) off.

HANDLES (MAKE 2)

Using 15.00mm (US 19) needles and A, cast on 21 sts.

Starting with a knit row, work 10 rows in St st from chart B, ending with a WS row.

Cast (bind) off.

BUTTON COVERS (MAKE 4)

Using 4.00mm (US 6) needles and G, cast on 8 sts.

Starting with a knit row, work in St st, inc 1 st at each end of 3rd and foll 2 alt rows (14 sts).

Work 5 rows, ending with a WS row.

Dec 1 st at each end of next and foll 2 alt rows (8 sts).

Work 1 row.

Cast (bind) off.

FINISHING

Sew in all loose ends, block and press. From lining fabric, cut out same size pieces as knitted Sides and Gusset, adding seam allowance along all edges. At cast (bound) off end of Gusset, join central row-end edges for last 5 rows. Join cast-on edge to cast (bound) off edges to form one long loop. Matching markers and gusset seam to corners of Sides, sew Gusset to outer edges of both Sides.

Make up lining fabric in same way as knitted sections. Slip lining inside Bag, turn under raw edges around opening along upper edge and neatly slip stitch in place.

Fold Handles in half and join cast-on edge to cast (bound) off edge to form a tube. Fold Handle flat, with seam running centrally along back of tube and sew ends closed. Using photograph as a guide, sew Handles to top of Sides, positioning ends of Handles approx. 10cm (4in) apart.

Following manufacturer's instructions, cover buttons with knitted Button Covers. Attach completed buttons to ends of Handles as in photograph.

If desired, attach decorative brooch to one Side between ends of Handles, as in photograph.

Chart A

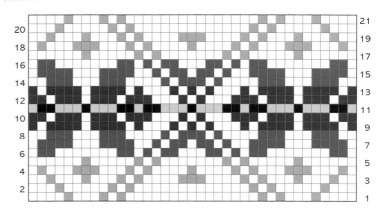

Chart B

Key

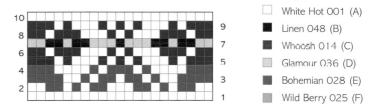

- ☐ White Hot 001 (A)
- ■ Linen 048 (B)
- ■ Whoosh 014 (C)
- ■ Glamour 036 (D)
- ■ Bohemian 028 (E)
- ■ Wild Berry 025 (F)

TIP

If you prefer, you can cover the buttons with circles of fabric. Choose a plain colour to complement your yarn choices and cover the buttons according to the instructions that come with your kit.

DESIGNED BY

Little bling bag

With this cute bag swinging from your arm, you are all set for summer parties. It's quick to crochet, so why not make several in colours to match your favourite party frocks and line and embellish them to suit.

YARN

Alchemy *Silk Purse* (100% silk), approx. 50g (1¾oz)/149m (163yd) per skein

   1 skein of Diamonda 09C

NEEDLES

4.50mm (G/6) crochet hook

5.00mm (H/8) crochet hook

EXTRAS

Piece of lining fabric 45cm (17½in) by 20cm (8in)

80cm (31½in) of 15-mm (⅝-in) wide ribbon

Twelve 6-mm (¼-in) diameter pearl beads

Matching sewing thread

TENSION (GAUGE)

17 sts and 21 rows = 10cm (4in) square measured over dc (sc) fabric and 4.50mm (G/6) hook

MEASUREMENTS

Completed bag is 19cm (7½in) wide (at widest point) and 13cm (5in) tall.

SKILL LEVEL

Intermediate

MAIN SECTION

Using 4.50mm (G/6) hook, make 44 ch and join with a ss (sl st) to form a ring.

Round 1: 1 ch (does NOT count as st), 1 dc (sc) into each ch to end, ss (sl st) to first dc (sc) (44 sts).

Round 2: 1 ch (does NOT count as st), 1 dc (sc) into each dc (sc) to end, ss (sl st) to first dc (sc).

Rounds 3 and 4: As round 2.

Round 5: 1 ch (does NOT count as st), 3 dc (sc) into first dc (sc), 1 dc (sc) into each of next 21 dc (sc), 3 dc (sc) into next dc (sc), 1 dc (sc) into each of last 21 dc (sc), ss (sl st) to first dc (sc) (48 sts).

Round 6: 1 ch (does NOT count as st), 2 dc (sc) into each of first 3 dc (sc), 1 dc (sc) into each of next 21 dc (sc), 2 dc (sc) into each of next 3 dc (sc), 1 dc (sc) into each of last 21 dc (sc), ss (sl st) to first dc (sc) (54 sts).

Round 7: 1 ch (does NOT count as st), 2 dc (sc) into each of first 6 dc (sc), 1 dc (sc) into each of next 21 dc (sc), 2 dc (sc) into each of next 6 dc (sc), 1 dc (sc) into each of last 21 dc (sc), ss (sl st) to first dc (sc) (66 sts).

Change to 5.00mm (H/8) crochet hook. Now rep round 2 until work measures 12cm (4¾in) from foundation ch edge.

Next round: 1 ch (does NOT count as st), *[miss 1 dc (sc), 1 dc (sc) in next dc (sc)] 6 times, 1 dc (sc) into each of next 21 dc (sc); rep from * once more, ss to first dc (sc) (54 sts).

Next round: As round 2.

Next round: 1 ch (does NOT count as st), *[miss 1 dc (sc), 1 dc (sc) in next dc (sc)] 3 times, 1 dc (sc) into each of next 21 dc (sc); rep from * once more, ss (sl st) to first dc (sc) (48 sts).

With RS together, fold Main Section in half and close base seam by working a row of dc (sc) through sts of both layers. Fasten off.

HANDLES (MAKE 2)

Using 4.50mm (G/6) hook, make 51 ch.

Row 1: 1 dc (sc) into 2nd ch from hook, 1 dc (sc) into each ch to end, turn (50 sts).

Row 2: 1 ch (does NOT count as st), 1 dc (sc) into each dc (sc) to end. Fasten off.

FINISHING

Sew in all loose ends, block and press the pieces.

From lining fabric, cut two pieces same size as Main Section, adding seam allowance along all edges. Sew the two lining pieces together along side and lower edges, leaving upper (opening) edge open.

Cut lengths of ribbon same length as Handles and neatly sew these lengths of ribbon to Handles. Using photograph as a guide, sew Handles inside upper edge of Bag, positioning Handles approx. 8cm (3in) apart.

Slip lining inside Bag, turn under raw edge around opening edge and neatly sew in place. Attach beads to upper opening edge as in photograph, spacing beads evenly along edge. Tie the remaining length of ribbon into a bow and attach to front of Bag.

TIP

Choosing a ribbon in the same pattern as the lining fabric, as here, is a great finishing touch. Look for polka dot and gingham deigns as you can often find ribbons and fabric in similar colours in these patterns.

DESIGNED BY

Fiona McTague

Inca satchel

Taking inspiration from traditional designs, but working them in today's colour palette, this satchel-style bag uses both intarsia and Fair Isle techniques, so it's a must for lovers of colour knitting.

YARN

Rowan Classic *Baby Alpaca DK* (100% baby alpaca), approx. 50g (1¾oz)/100m (109yd) per ball

    4 balls of Jacob 205 (A)

    2 balls of Lincoln 209 (B)

    1 ball of Southdown 208 (C)

NEEDLES

Pair of 3.25mm (US 3) knitting needles

Pair of 3.75mm (US 5) knitting needles

EXTRAS

Three 15-mm (⅝-in) diameter buttons

TENSION (GAUGE)

24 sts and 36 rows = 10cm (4in) square measured over patt using 3.75mm (US 5) needles

MEASUREMENTS

Completed bag is 30cm (11¾in) wide, 22cm (8½in) tall and 5cm (2in) deep.

SKILL LEVEL

Advanced

Chart A

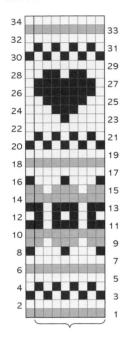

Key

☐ Jacob 205 (A)

■ Lincoln 209 (B)

▨ Southdown 208 (C)

BACK AND FRONT (BOTH ALIKE)

Using 3.75mm (US 5) needles and A, cast on 71 sts.

Work in garter st for 2 rows, ending with a WS row.

Joining in and breaking off colours as required, stranding yarn not in use loosely across WS of work, reading odd-numbered rows as knit rows from right to left and even-numbered rows as purl rows from left to right, now work in patt from chart A as follows:

Row 3 (RS): With A k3, work edge st of chart, then rep the 8-st patt rep 8 times, with A k3.

Row 4: With A k3, rep the 8-st patt rep of chart 8 times, work edge st, with A k3.

These 2 rows set the sts – central 65 sts in Fair Isle patt from chart with 3 sts at each end of every row in garter st with A.

Keeping sts correct as now set and working appropriate rows of chart, work chart rows 3–34, then chart rows 1–34 again, ending with a WS row.

Cut off contrasts and cont with A only.

Change to 3.25mm (US 3) needles.

Work in garter st for 6 rows, ending with a WS row.

Cast (bind) off.

FLAP

Using 3.25mm (US 3) needles and A, cast on 70 sts.

Work in garter st for 2 rows, ending with a WS row.

Row 3 (RS): K5, *cast (bind) off 2 sts (to make a buttonhole), k until there are 27 sts on RH needle after cast (bind) off; rep from * once more, cast (bind) off 2 sts (to make third buttonhole), k to end.

Row 4: Knit to end, casting on 2 sts over those cast (bound) off on previous row.

Work in garter st for 2 rows more, ending with a WS row.

Change to 3.75mm (US 5) needles.

Row 7 (RS): Knit.

Row 8: K3, p to last 3 sts, k3.

Rows 9–10: As rows 7 and 8.

Joining in and breaking off B as required, stranding yarn not in use loosely across WS of work, reading odd-numbered rows as knit rows from right to left and even-numbered rows as purl rows from left to right, now work in patt from chart B as follows:

Row 11 (RS): With A k3, work next 64 sts as row 1 of chart B, with A k3.

Row 12: With A k3, work next 64 sts as row 2 of chart B, with A k3.

These 2 rows set the sts – central 64 sts in Fair Isle patt from chart with 3 sts at

each end of every row in garter st with A. Keeping sts correct as now set and working appropriate rows of chart, work chart rows 3–30, ending with a WS row.

Cut off B and cont with A only.

Now rep rows 7 and 8 until Flap measures 22cm (8½in), ending with a WS row.

Cast (bind) off.

BASE

Using 3.75mm (US 5) needles and A, cast on 13 sts.

Row 1 (RS): Knit.

Row 2: K2, p9, k2.

Using a separate ball of yarn for each block of colour and twisting yarns together on WS where they meet to avoid holes forming, cont as follows:

Row 3: With A k6, with B k1, with A k6.

Row 4: With A k2, p3, with B p3, with A p3, k2.

Row 5: With A k4, with B k5, with A k4.

Row 6: With A k2, p1, with B p7, with A p1, k2.

Row 7: With A k3, with B k7, with A k3.

Row 8: With A k2, p2, with B p2, with A p1, with B p2, with A p2, k2.

These 8 rows form the patt.

Cont in patt for 82 rows more, ending after patt row 2 and with a WS row.

Cast (bind) off.

SIDE GUSSETS (MAKE 2)

Using 3.75mm (US 5) needles and A, cast on 13 sts.

Starting with patt row 1, work in patt as given for Base for 66 rows, ending after patt row 2 and with a WS row.

Cast (bind) off.

STRAP

Using 3.75mm (US 5) needles and A, cast on 13 sts.

Starting with patt row 1, work in patt as given for Base until Strap measures approx. 142cm (56in), ending after patt row 2 and with a WS row.

Cast (bind) off.

FINISHING

Sew in all loose ends, block and press the pieces.

Matching cast (bound) off and cast on edges, sew row-end edges of Gussets to row-end edges of Back and Front. Sew Base to cast on edges of Back, Front and Gussets. Sew cast (bound) off edge of Flap to cast (bound) off edge of Back. Sew cast on and cast (bound) off ends of Strap to cast (bound) off edges of Gussets. Sew buttons onto Front to correspond with buttonholes in Flap.

Chart B

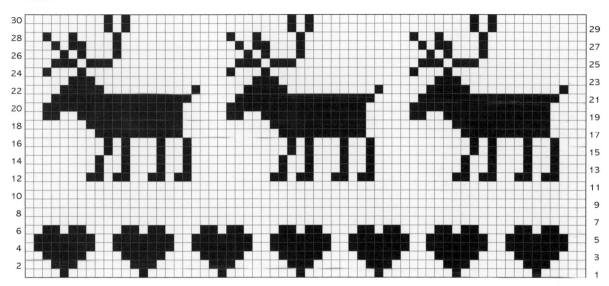

Key

☐ Jacob 205 (A)

■ Lincoln 209 (B)

▨ Southdown 208 (C)

DESIGNED BY

Flower trim bag

The perfect bag for carrying lots of stuff without compromising on casual style.
A wide, textured border defines the flap and contrasts beautifully with the soft,
felted look of the main yarn.

YARN

Rowan *Felted Tweed* (50% merino wool, 25% alpaca, 25%
viscose), approx. 50g (1¾oz)/175m (191yd) per ball

   2 balls of Carbon 159 (A)

Rowan Classic *Baby Alpaca DK* (100% baby alpaca), approx.
50g (1¾oz)/100m (109yd) per ball

   1 ball of Southdown 208 (B)

NEEDLES

Pair of 3.00mm (US 3) knitting needles
Pair of 3.75mm (US 5) knitting needles

EXTRAS

Stitch holders
Ten small black glass beads

TENSION (GAUGE)

23 sts and 32 rows = 10cm (4in) square measured over St st
using 3.75mm (US 5) needles and A

MEASUREMENTS

Completed bag is 30cm (11¾in) wide, 30cm (11¾in) tall
and 4cm (1½in) deep.

SKILL LEVEL

Intermediate

BACK

Using 3.75mm (US 5) needles and A, cast on 69 sts.

Row 1 (RS): Knit.

Row 2: K1, purl to last st, k1.

Rep these 2 rows until Back measures 30cm (11¾in), ending with a WS row. Cast (bind) off.

FRONT

Using 3.75mm (US 5) needles and A, cast on 69 sts.

Row 1 (RS): Knit.

Row 2: K1, purl to last st, k1.

Rep these 2 rows until Front measures 28.5cm (11¼in), ending with a WS row. Work in garter st for 6 rows, ending with a WS row.

Cast (bind) off.

GUSSET

Using 3.75mm (US 5) needles and A, cast on 10 sts.

Row 1 (RS): Knit.

Row 2: K1, purl to last st, k1.

These 2 rows form patt.

Cont in patt until Gusset fits down one row-end edge of Back, from cast (bound) off edge to cast on edge.

Place markers at both ends of last row. Cont in patt until Gusset, from markers, fits along cast on edge of Back.

Place markers at both ends of last row. Cont in patt until Gusset, from last pair of markers, fits up other row-end edge of Back to cast (bound) off edge, ending with a WS row.

Cast (bind) off.

STRAP

Using 3.75mm (US 5) needles and B, cast on 14 sts.

Row 1 (RS): K1, p12, k1.

Row 2: K1, *(k1, p1, k1) all into next st, p3tog; rep from * to last st, k1.

Row 3: K1, p12, k1.

Row 4: K1, *p3tog, (k1, p1, k1) all into next st; rep from * to last st, k1.

These 4 rows form patt.

Cont in patt until Strap measures

116cm (45½in), ending with a WS row.
Cast (bind) off.

FLAP

Using 3.75mm (US 5) needles and B,
cast on 86 sts.
Work in patt as given for Strap for 16
rows, ending with a WS row.
Next row (RS): Patt 13 sts, k1 and slip
these 14 sts onto a holder, [k4, k2tog] 9
times, k5, patt next 13 sts and slip last
14 sts onto another holder.
Rejoin A to rem centre 49 sts with
WS facing.
Starting with a purl row, work in St st
until Flap measures 30cm (11¾in) from
cast on edge, ending with a WS row.
Cast (bind) off.

FLAP EDGINGS (BOTH ALIKE)

Slip 14 sts from holder onto 3.75mm
(US 5) needles and rejoin B with
WS facing.
Cont in patt as set until Edging, when
slightly stretched, fits up row-end edge
of central section of Flap to cast
(bound) off edge, ending with a WS row.
Cast (bind) off.
Work other side in exactly the same way.

FLOWER PETALS

Using 3.00mm (US 3) needles and B,
cast on 9 sts.

Row 1 (RS): K1, *p1, k1; rep from *
to end.
**Row 2: As row 1.
These 2 rows form moss (seed) st.
Keeping moss (seed) st correct, cont
as follows:
Row 3: K1, m1, moss (seed) st to end
(10 sts).
Work 1 row.
Rep last 2 rows once more (11 sts).
Work 2 rows without shaping.
Row 9: K2tog tbl, moss (seed) st to end
(10 sts).
Work 1 row.
Rep last 2 rows once more (9 sts).
Cast (bind) off 4 sts at beg of next row
(5 sts).
Work 1 row.****
Cast on 4 sts at beg of next row
(9 sts).***
Rep from ** to *** 4 times more, then
from ** to **** again.
Cast (bind) off rem 5 sts.

FLOWER CENTRE

Using 3.00mm (US 3) needles and A,
cast on 3 sts.
Row 1 (RS): K3.
Row 2 and every foll alt row: Purl.
Row 3: K1, [m1, k1] twice (5 sts).
Row 5: K1, m1, k3, m1, k1 (7 sts).
Row 7: K2tog, k3, k2tog (5 sts).
Row 9: K2tog, k1, k2tog (3 sts).
Row 10: P3.
Cast (bind) off.

FINISHING

Sew in all loose ends. Block and press
pieces worked in St st **only**.
Matching cast on and cast (bound) off
ends of Gusset to cast (bound) off edges
of Front and Back, and Gusset markers
to ends of cast on edges of Front and
Back, sew Gusset to Front and Back
along cast on and row-end edges.
Neatly slip stitch Flap Edgings to
sides of Flap, then sew entire cast
(bound) off edge of Flap and Flap
Edgings to cast (bound) off edge of
Back. Sew ends of Strap to ends of
Gusset as in photograph.
Join cast on and cast (bound) off
ends of Flower Petals. Run gathering
threads around straight row-end edge
and pull up to form flower. Sew Flower
Centre in place at centre of Flower
Petals. Sew completed flower to Flap as
in photograph, attaching beads to
Flower Centre.

DESIGNED BY

Carol Meldrum

Shoulder bag

For this bag you need to make your own chunky yarn – and it's so simple to do.
Knitted on big needles, the bag will grow quickly and uses only the simplest
stitches, perfect for a knitting and crochet novice.

YARN

Rowan printed cotton fabric (100% cotton), approx. 115cm
(45in) wide

   3.50m of shaggy poppy PJ03 (A)

Rowan *Handknit Cotton* (100% cotton), approx. 50g
(1¾oz)/85m (93yd) per ball

   2 balls of Thunder 335 (B)

NEEDLES

Pair of 10.00mm (US 15) knitting needles

4.00mm (G/6) crochet hook

TENSION (GAUGE)

8 sts and 10 rows = 10cm (4in) square measured over St st
using A and 10.00mm (US 15) needles.

MEASUREMENTS

Completed bag is 39cm (15½in) wide, 30cm (11¾in) tall
and 11cm (4¼in) deep.

SKILL LEVEL

Beginner

SPECIAL NOTE

Before starting to knit Bag, fabric (A) needs to be cut into strips to make the knitting yarn. Starting at first cut end, cut along length of fabric approx. 2.5cm (1in) from selvedge, stopping approx. 2.5cm (1in) from second cut end. Starting at second cut end, cut along fabric again approx. 2.5cm (1in) from first cut, again stopping approx. 2.5cm (1in) from opposite end. Continue in this way to make one continuous long length approx. 2.5cm (1in) wide and wind fabric into a ball. (Note: 'corners' at ends of cuts will be wider than rest of strip but this adds to the uneven nature of the knitted fabric.)

SIDES (MAKE 2)

Using 10.00mm (US 15) needles and A, cast on 31 sts.
Starting with a knit row, work in St st for 30 rows, ending with a WS row.
Cast (bind) off purlwise (on RS).

SIDE GUSSETS AND BASE

Using 10.00mm (US 15) needles and A, cast on 3 sts.
Starting with a knit row, work in St st as follows:
Work 2 rows, ending with a WS row.
Row 3 (RS): K1, [m1, k1] twice (5 sts).
Work 3 rows.

Row 7: K1, m1, k to last st, m1, k1
(7 sts).
Rep last 4 rows once more (9 sts).
Work 4 rows, ending with a RS row.
Row 16 (WS): Knit (to form fold line at
base of first side gusset section).
Starting again with a knit row, work in
St st for 41 rows, ending with a RS row.
Row 58 (WS): Knit (to form fold line at
base of second side gusset section –
section between fold lines is base).
Starting again with a knit row, cont in
St st as follows:
Work 4 rows, ending with a WS row.
Row 63 (RS): K1, skpo, k to last 3 sts,
k2tog, k1 (7 sts).
Work 3 rows.
Rep last 4 rows once more (5 sts).
Row 71: K1, sl 1, k2tog, psso, k1
(3 sts).
Work 3 rows, ending with a WS row.
Cast (bind) off.

STRAP

Using 4.00mm (G/6) crochet hook and
B, make 11 ch.
Row 1: 1 tr (dc) into 4th ch from hook,
1 tr (dc) into each ch to end, turn
(9 sts).
Row 2: 3 ch (counts as first tr (dc)),
miss tr (dc) at base of 3 ch, 1 tr (dc) into
each tr (dc) to end, working last tr (dc)
into top of 3 ch at beg of prev row, turn.

Rep last row until Strap measures
275cm (108¼in).
Fasten off.

FINISHING

Sew in all loose ends, block and press
the pieces.
Matching fold lines of Side Gussets and
Base to ends of cast on edge of Sides,
sew Side Gussets and Base to Sides –
sew pieces together with WS facing so
seams form a ridge on outside of Bag
and position cast on and cast (bound)
off ends of Gusset sections approx.
15cm (6in) below cast (bound) off
edges of Sides. Sew Sides together
above tops of Gusset sections.
Join short ends of Strap to form one
large loop. Using photograph as a guide,
wrap Strap around Bag, positioning
sections of Strap approx. 13cm (5in)
apart. Sew Strap securely in place
across upper opening edges, base and
midway up Sides.

TIP

All sorts of fabrics can be made into
yarn, though it's best to avoid fabric
that frays very readily, like silk. Also,
heavy fabrics, such as corduroy, can
be too stiff and thick when knitted
up. If you are recycling old
garments, you don't have to worry
about small stains as they won't
show in the finished knitting, though
worn areas might break when cut
into thin strips. Fabric knitting is a
great way of giving a much-loved
but now unfashionable dress a new
lease of life.

DESIGNED BY

Sue Bradley

Black and white evening bag

Whether you are going to a smart wedding, a classy cocktail party or on a special night out with the girls, this little bag is the perfect accessory. It's quick to knit and you can choose colours and trims to match your outfit.

YARN

Rowan Classic *Cashcotton DK* (35% cotton, 25% polyamide, 18% angora, 13% viscose, 9% cashmere), approx. 50g (1¾oz)/130m (142yd) per ball

  1 ball of White 600 (A)

  1 ball of Black 607 (B)

NEEDLES

Pair of 3.25mm (US 3) knitting needles

Pair of 4.00mm (US 6) knitting needles

3.25mm (D/3) crochet hook

EXTRAS

Five different fancy black buttons – four 2-cm (¾-in) diameter buttons (for handles) and one 15-mm (⅝-in) diameter button for flower centre

90 (35½in) of 5-cm (2-in) wide black lace

11 black sequins

Piece of lining fabric 45cm (17¾in) by 30cm (11¾in)

Matching sewing thread

TENSION (GAUGE)

22 sts and 30 rows = 10cm (4in) square measured over St st using 4.00mm (US 6) needles

MEASUREMENTS

Completed bag is 20cm (8in) wide and 24cm (9½in) tall.

SKILL LEVEL

Intermediate

MAIN SECTION

Using 3.25mm (US 3) needles and B, cast on 88 sts.

Row 1 (RS): *K1, p1; rep from * to end.
Row 2: *P1, k1; rep from * to end.
These 2 rows form moss (seed) st.
Work in moss (seed) st for 6 rows more, ending with a WS row.
Cut off B and join in A.
Change to 4.00mm (US 6) needles.
Starting with a knit row, work in St st until Main Section measures 24cm (9½in) from cast on edge, ending with a RS row.
Cast (bind) off.

HANDLES (MAKE 2)

Using 3.25mm (US 3) needles and B, cast on 8 sts.
Work in moss (seed) st as given for Main Section for 30cm (11¾in), ending with a RS row.
Cast (bind) off.

FLOWER

Using 3.25mm (D/3) crochet hook and A, make 6 ch and join with a ss (sl st) to form a ring.

Round 1: 1 ch (does NOT count as st), 1 dc (sc) into ring, *(1 tr (dc), 1 dtr (tr) , 4 ch and 1 dc (sc)) into ring; rep from * 5 times more, replacing dc (sc) at end of last rep with ss (sl st) to first dc (sc) (6 petals).

Round 2: [4 ch (keeping this ch behind petals of prev round), 1 ss (sl st) into next dc (sc)] 6 times, working last ss (sl st) into same place as ss (sl st) at end of prev round.

Round 3: 1 ch (does NOT count as st), (1 dc (sc), 1 tr (dc), 1 dtr (tr) , 4 ch, 1 dc (sc), 1 tr (dc), 1 dtr (tr) , 4 ch and 1 dc (sc)) into each ch sp to end, ss (sl st) to first dc (sc) (12 petals).

Round 4: [5 ch (keeping this ch behind petals of prev round), miss 1 dc (sc), 1 ss (sl st) into next dc (sc)] 6 times, working last ss (sl st) into same place as ss (sl st) at end of prev round.

Round 5: 1 ch (does NOT count as st), (1 dc (sc), 8 ch, 1 dc (sc) and 8 ch) into each ch sp to last ch sp, 1 dc (sc) into last ch sp, 4 ch, 1 tr (dc) into first dc (sc) (11 ch sps).

Round 6: 3 ch (counts as first tr (dc)), 1 tr (dc) into ch sp partly formed by tr (dc) at end of prev round, *4 ch**, (2 tr (dc), 2 ch and 2 tr (dc)) into next ch sp; rep from * to end, ending last rep at **, 2 tr (dc) into same ch sp as used at beg of round, 2 ch, ss (sl st) to top of 3 ch at beg of round.

Round 7: 1 ch (does NOT count as st), 1 dc (sc) into st at base of 1 ch, 1 dc (sc) into next tr (dc), *(2 dc (sc), 6 ch and 2 dc (sc)) into next ch sp, 1 dc (sc) into each of next 2 tr (dc), 2 dc (sc) into next ch sp**, 1 dc (sc) into each of next 2 tr (dc); rep from * to end, ending last rep at **, ss (sl st) to first dc (sc). Fasten off.

FINISHING

Sew in all loose ends, block and press the knitted pieces.

From lining fabric, cut out same size piece as knitted Main Section, adding seam allowance along all edges.

Cut lace into two equal lengths. Using photograph as a guide, sew lace across knitted Main Section – one strip just below moss (seed) st section and other strip just above cast (bound) off edge. Fold Main Section in half and sew side (row-end edge) and base (cast (bound) off edge) seam.

Sew Handles to each side around upper edge so that ends of Handles are on RS of moss (seed) st upper band and positioning Handles approx. 7.5cm (3in) apart. Sew one of the larger buttons onto each Handle end.

Sew Flower onto one side of Bag as in photograph, attaching the smaller button at the centre. Sew a sequin onto each group of 4 tr (dc) around Flower. Make up lining in same way as knitted Main Section. Slip lining inside Bag, turn under raw edge around upper opening edge and neatly slip stitch in place.

TIP

To attach the lace pieces, first pin them in position. Use the grid formed by the stitches and rows of the knitted fabric to make sure that the pieces are straight. Use a sewing thread that matches the lace, not the yarn, and a fine hand-sewing needle. Make tiny slip stitches, going just over the edge of the lace, then through the knitted fabric. Follow the shaped edge of the lace accurately, being careful not to pull it out of shape. If the shaped edge is quite fancy, you may find it easier to quickly tack it in place first before slip stitching it.

DESIGNED BY

Fair Isle tote

Zesty, contemporary colours bring traditional Fair Isle right into the 21st century and make this bag a modern classic. The rib top and looping straps add understated detailing that complements the design.

YARN

Rowan *Pure Wool DK* (100% superwash wool), approx. 50g (1¾oz)/125m (136yd) per ball

  3 balls of Hay 014 (A)

  1 ball of Barley 015 (B)

  1 ball of Avocado 019 (C)

  1 ball of Shale 002 (D)

  1 ball of Damson 030 (E)

  1 ball of Kiss 036 (F)

  1 ball of Glade 021 (G)

NEEDLES

Pair of 3.25mm (US 3) knitting needles

Pair of 4.00mm (US 6) knitting needles

TENSION (GAUGE)

24 sts and 32 rows = 10cm (4in) square measured over patt using 4.00mm (US 6) needles

MEASUREMENTS

Completed bag is 30cm (11¾in) wide and 36cm (14in) tall.

SKILL LEVEL

Intermediate

SIDES (MAKE 2)

Using 4.00mm (US 6) needles and A, cast on 73 sts.

Starting with a knit row, repeating the 8-st patt rep 9 times across rows and working edge st as indicated, work in St st from chart as follows:

Work all 30 rows of chart 3 times, then chart rows 1–4 again, inc 1 st at centre of last row and ending with a WS row (74 sts).

Cut off contrasts and cont with A only.

Change to 3.25mm (US 3) needles.

Next row (RS): K2, *p2, k2; rep from * to end.

Next row: P2, *k2, p2; rep from * to end.

These 2 rows form rib.

Work in rib for 6 rows more, ending with a WS row.

Next row (RS): Rib 12, cast (bind) off 2 sts (to form eyelet hole for Strap), rib to last 14 sts, cast (bind) off 2 sts (to form other eyelet hole for Strap), rib to end.

Next row: Rib to end, casting on 2 sts over those cast (bound) off on previous row.

Work in rib for 8 rows more, ending with a WS row.

Cast (bind) off in rib.

STRAPS (MAKE 2)

Using 3.25mm (US 3) needles and A,
cast on 6 sts.

Starting with a knit row, work in St st
until Strap measures 128cm (50½in),
ending with a WS row.

Cast (bind) off.

FINISHING

Sew in all loose ends, block and press
the pieces.

Join the Sides along cast on and row-
end edges.

Starting on RS of work, take one end of
one Strap through one eyelet hole on
one side, then take other end of same
Strap through other eyelet hole of same
Side. Join ends of Strap. Thread ends
of other Strap through eyelet holes of
other Side and join ends in same way.
(Straps will roll in on themselves to form
soft tubes.)

> ### TIP
>
> If you decide to line this bag with
> fabric, follow the principle described
> in Little Bling Bag, page 54, but turn
> under the top edge of the lining so
> that it lies just below the ribbed top
> of the knitted bag before sewing it
> in place.

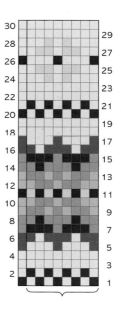

Key

- ☐ Hay 014 (A)
- ▨ Barley 015 (B)
- ☐ Avocado 019 (C)
- ▨ Shale 002 (D)
- ■ Damson 030 (E)
- ■ Kiss 036 (F)
- ▨ Glade 021 (G)

DESIGNED BY

Judy Furlong

Golden shell bag

Unashamedly feminine, this delicate bag has a knitted lining as well as a lace knit outer, so it's as practical as it is pretty. Pearls decorate this version, but you could use crystal beads that tone with your dress.

YARN

Louisa Harding *Glisten* (97% nylon, 3% polyester), approx. 50g (1¾oz)/85m (93yd) per ball
   1 ball of gold 4 (A)
Louisa Harding *Nautical Cotton* (100% mercerised cotton), approx. 50g (1¾oz)/85m (93yd) per ball
   1 ball of black 15 (B)

NEEDLES

Pair of 3.75mm (US 5) knitting needles
Pair of 4.50mm (US 7) knitting needles
3.00mm (D/3) crochet hook

EXTRAS

Small amount of waste yarn (for cast on edges)
10cm (4in) zip
3 pearl beads

TENSION (GAUGE)

20 sts and 29 rows = 10cm (4in) square measured over patt using 4.50mm (US 7) needles and A
20 sts and 28 rows = 10cm (4in) square measured over St st using 4.50mm (US 7) needles and B

MEASUREMENTS

Completed bag is 22cm (8½in) wide (at widest point) and 15cm (6in) deep.

SKILL LEVEL

Advanced

OUTER SECTION

Using 4.50mm (US 7) needles and waste yarn, cast on 26 sts.
Purl one row.
Cut off waste yarn and join in A.

Row 1 (RS): Knit.

Now work in patt as follows:

Row 2 (WS): K1, *yfwd, k2tog; rep from * to last st, k1.

Row 3: P1, *yrn, p2tog; rep from * to last st, p1.

Row 4: As row 2.

Row 5: Slip first st purlwise with yarn at front (RS) of work, then take yarn to back (WS) of work (thereby twisting slipped st), m1, knit to end (27 sts).

Row 6: Purl.

Row 7: Slip first st purlwise with yarn at front (RS) of work, then take yarn to back (WS) of work, m1, k17, wrap next st (by bringing yarn to front of work, slipping next st from LH needle onto RH needle, taking yarn back to back of work and then slipping same st back onto LH needle – when working back across wrapped sts work the wrapped st and the wrapping loop together as though they were one st) and turn.

Row 8: Purl.

Row 9: Slip first st purlwise with yarn at front (RS) of work, then take yarn to back (WS) of work, m1, k9, wrap next st and turn.

Row 10: Purl.

Row 11: Slip first st purlwise with yarn at front (RS) of work, then take yarn to back (WS) of work, k to end (29 sts).

Row 12: Purl.

Row 13: Slip first st purlwise with yarn at front (RS) of work, then take yarn to back (WS) of work, k2tog, k8, wrap next st and turn.

Row 14: Purl.

Row 15: Slip first st purlwise with yarn at front (RS) of work, then take yarn to back (WS) of work, k2tog, k16, wrap next st and turn.

Row 16: Purl.

Row 17: Slip first st purlwise with yarn at front (RS) of work, then take yarn to back (WS) of work, k2tog, k to end (27 sts).

Last 16 rows form patt.

Rows 18–65: As rows 2–17, 3 times.

Rows 66–68: As rows 2–4.

Row 69: Knit.

Row 70 (WS): Knit (to form fold line for side of Bag).

Place marker at upper (straight) edge of last row.

Row 71: Knit.

Rows 72–135: As rows 2–17, 4 times.

Rows 136–138: As rows 2–4.

Row 139: Knit.

Row 140 (WS): Knit (to form fold line for other side of Bag).

Place marker at upper (straight) edge of last row.

Slip sts of first row in A onto a spare needle, carefully unravelling waste yarn. Fold Main Section in half with RS together and cast (bind) off both sets of sts (those of row 140 and those just slipped onto spare needle) together by taking one st from first needle together with corresponding st from other needle.

OUTER UPPER BORDERS (BOTH ALIKE)

Using 3.75mm (US 5) needles, with RS facing and A, pick up and knit 36 sts along first section of straight row-end edge of Outer Section between markers at ends of fold lines.

Row 1 (WS): K1, *yfwd, k2tog; rep from * to last st, k1.
Row 2: P1, *yrn, p2tog; rep from * to last st, p1.
Row 3: As row 1.
Rows 4–5: Knit.
Cast (bind) off.
Work second Upper Border in exactly the same way but do NOT fasten off last cast (bound) off st.
Slip this last loop onto 3.00mm (D/3) crochet hook and make a ch 25cm (10in) long, work a ss (sl st) into first cast (bound) off st of other Upper Border and fasten off.

INNER SECTION
Using 4.50mm (US 7) needles and waste yarn, cast on 24 sts.
Purl one row.
Cut off waste yarn and join in B.
Row 1 (RS): Knit.
Now work in patt as follows:
Row 2 (WS): Purl.
Row 3: Knit.
Row 4: Purl.
Row 5: Sl 1, m1, k to end (25 sts).
Row 6: Purl.
Row 7: Sl 1, m1, k15, wrap next st and turn.
Row 8: Purl.
Row 9: Sl 1, m1, k7, wrap next st and turn.

Row 10: Purl.
Row 11: Sl 1, k to end (27 sts).
Row 12: Purl.
Row 13: Sl 1, k2tog, k6, wrap next st and turn.
Row 14: Purl.
Row 15: Sl 1, k2tog, k14, wrap next st and turn.
Row 16: Purl.
Row 17: Slip first st purlwise with yarn at front (RS) of work, then take yarn to back (WS) of work, k2tog, k to end (24 sts).
Last 16 rows form patt.
Rows 18–65: As rows 2–17, 3 times.
Rows 66–68: As rows 2–4.
Row 69 (WS): Knit (to form fold line for side of Bag).
Place marker at straight edge of last row.
Rows 70–133: As rows 2–17, 4 times.
Rows 134–136: As rows 2–4.
Slip sts of first row in B onto a spare needle, carefully unravelling waste yarn. Fold Inner Section in half with RS together and cast (bind) off both sets of sts (those of row 136 and those just slipped onto spare needle) together by taking one st from first needle together with corresponding st from other needle.

INNER UPPER BORDERS (BOTH ALIKE)
Using 3.75mm (US 5) needles, with WS facing and B, pick up and knit 32 sts along first section of straight row-end edge of Inner Section between marker and seam.
Row 1: Purl.
Cast (bind) off.
Work second Upper Border in exactly the same way.

FINISHING
Sew in all loose ends, block and press the pieces.
Sew shaped base seam of Outer Section, then sew shaped base seam of Inner Section.
Insert zip into opening edge of Inner Section. Slip Inner Section inside Outer Section and sew together around upper edge, stitching along pick-up row of Outer Upper Borders.
Thread beads onto strong sewing thread and attach to zip pull as in photograph.

DESIGNED BY

Judy Furlong

Stripy bag

Self-striping yarn is marvellous stuff, allowing you to concentrate on shaping and stitch detail while the colour patterning takes care of itself. This big bag makes the most of the yarn with varying-width stripes on different sections.

YARN

Twilleys *Freedom Spirit* (100% pure new wool), approx. 50g (1¾oz)/120m (131yd) per ball

   6 balls of Essence 507 (A)

Twilleys *Freedom Wool* (100% pure new wool), approx. 50g (1¾oz)/50m (54yd) per ball

   2 balls of navy 423 (B)

NEEDLES

Pair of 4.00mm (US 6) knitting needles

Pair of 6.50mm (US 10½) knitting needles

Two 6.50mm (US 10½) double-pointed needles

Two cable needles

EXTRAS

30cm (12in) zip

Piece of buckram 12cm (4¾in) by 52cm (20½in)

Matching sewing thread

TENSION (GAUGE)

22 sts and 28 rows = 10cm (4in) square measured over St st using 4.00mm (US 6) needles and A

25 sts and 34 rows = 10cm (4in) square measured over patt using 6.50mm (US 10½) needles and A

MEASUREMENTS

Completed bag is 46cm (18in) wide, 25cm (10in) tall (excluding strap) and 12cm (4¾in) deep.

SKILL LEVEL

Advanced

SIDES (MAKE 2)

Using 4.00mm (US 6) needles and A, cast on 86 sts.

Place markers at both ends of cast on edge.

Starting with a knit row, cont in St st as follows:

Inc 1 st at each end of next 7 rows, then on foll 4th row (102 sts).

Place markers at both ends of last row.

Work 75 rows, ending with a WS row.

Next row (RS): K13, *slip next 3 sts onto a cable needle, then foll 3 sts onto second cable needle, fold work so that cable needles and LH needle form a 'Z' shape, knit tog first st from first cable needle with last st from second cable needle and first st from LH needle, knit tog centre sts from both cable needles with next st from LH needle, knit tog last st from first cable needle with first st on second cable needle and next st on LH needle – first half of pleat completed, slip next 3 sts onto a cable needle, then foll 3 sts onto second cable needle, fold work so that cable needles and LH needle form an 'S' shape, knit tog first st from LH needle with last st from second cable needle and first st from first cable needle, knit tog next st from LH needle with centre sts from both cable needles, knit tog next st on LH needle with first st from second cable needle and last st on

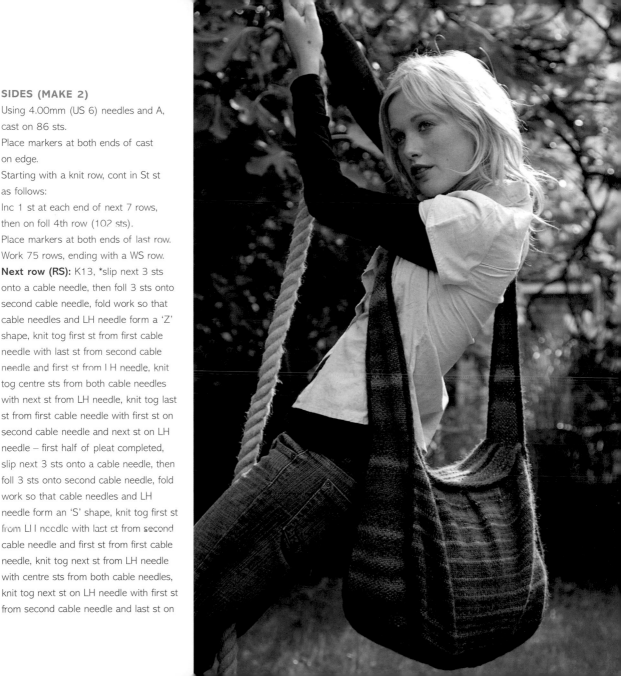

first cable needle – second half of pleat completed*, k11, rep from * to * once more – second pleat completed, k11, rep from * to * once more – third pleat completed, k13 (66 sts).

Place markers at both ends of last row.

SHAPE TOP GUSSET

Change to 6.50mm (US 10½) needles.

Now work in patt as follows:

Row 1 (WS): *P1, take yarn to back (RS) of work, slip next st purlwise, bring yarn to front (WS) of work; rep from * to end.

Row 2: *K1, bring yarn to front (RS) of work, slip next st purlwise, take yarn to back (WS) of work; rep from * to end.

These 2 rows form patt.

Work in patt for 8 rows more, ending with a RS row.

Change to 4.00mm (US 6) needles.

Next row (WS): With RH needle point, pick up loop of first st of last marked row and place on LH needle, p this loop tog with first st on LH needle (forming small ridge on RS of work), *pick up loop of next st of marked row and place on LH needle, p this loop tog with next st on LH needle; rep from * to end.

Change to 6.50mm (US 10½) needles.

Starting with row 2, work in patt for 12 rows, ending with a WS row.

Cast (bind) off.

GUSSET AND STRAP

Using 6.50mm (US 10½) needles and A, cast on 30 sts.

Starting with row 2, work in patt as given for top gusset for 68 rows, ending with a WS row.

Place markers at both ends of last row – these markers match markers at ends of cast on edge of Sides.

Work 20 rows.

Place markers at both ends of last row – these markers match markers at top of shaped row-end edges of Sides.

Work 28 rows, ending with a WS row.

Keeping patt correct, dec 1 st at each end of next and 2 foll 28th rows (24 sts).

Work 9 rows.

Place markers at both ends of last row – these markers match to ridges of Sides at start of top gusset.

Work 18 rows, ending with a WS row.

Keeping patt correct, dec 1 st at each end of next and every foll 28th row until 14 sts rem.

Work 63 rows.

Inc 1 st at each end of next and every foll 28th row until there are 24 sts, taking inc sts into patt.

Work 17 rows.

Place markers at both ends of last row – last section forms strap and these markers match to other end of ridges of Sides at start of top gusset.

Work 10 rows.

Inc 1 st at each end of next and 2 foll 28th rows (30 sts).

Work 27 rows, ending with a WS row.

Place markers at both ends of last row – these markers match markers at top of other shaped row-end edges of Sides.

Work 20 rows.

Place markers at both ends of last row – these markers match markers at other ends of cast on edge of Sides.

Work 68 rows, ending with a WS row.

Cast (bind) off.

FINISHING

Sew in all loose ends, block and press the pieces.

Insert zip between cast (bound) off edges of Top Gusset sections.

Join cast on and cast (bound) off edges of Gusset and Strap to form one large loop. Matching appropriate markers and gusset seam to centre of cast on edge of Sides, sew Gusset to cast on and row-end edges of Sides, leaving strap section free. Sew row-end edges of top gussets in place across strap.

PIPING

Using 6.50mm (US 10½) dpns and B, cast on 3 sts.

Row 1: K3, *without turning work slip these 3 sts to opposite end of needle and bring yarn to opposite end of work pulling it quite tightly across WS of work, now knit these 3 sts again; rep from * until piping fits around entire row-end edge of Gusset and Strap.

Cast (bind) off.

Join ends of Piping, then neatly sew in place as in photograph.

Make and attach a second length of Piping in exactly the same way.

Insert buckram into base of Bag, trimming it to fit as necessary, and carefully sew in place.

TIP

This bag would also look fabulous knitted in different shades of one plain colour. Try using one shade for the sides, a second for the gusset and strap section and a third shade for the piping.

Knitting

TENSION (GAUGE) AND SELECTING CORRECT NEEDLE SIZE

Tension (gauge) can differ quite dramatically between knitters. This is because of the way that the needles and the yarn are held. So if your tension (gauge) does not match that stated in the pattern, you should change your needle size following this simple rule:

- If your knitting is too loose, your tension (gauge) will read that you have fewer stitches and rows than the given tension (gauge), and you will need to change to a smaller needle to make the stitch size smaller.

- If your knitting is too tight, your tension (gauge) will read that you have more stitches and rows than the given tension (gauge), and you will need to change to a thicker needle to make the stitch size bigger.

Please note that if the projects in this book are not knitted to the correct tension (gauge), yarn quantities will be affected.

KNITTING A TENSION (GAUGE) SWATCH

No matter how excited you are about a new knitting project, take time to knit a tension (gauge) swatch for accurate sizing. Use the same needles, yarn and stitch pattern as those that will be used for the main work and knit a sample at least 12.5cm (5in) square. Smooth out the finished piece on a flat surface, but do not stretch it.

To check the stitch tension (gauge), place a ruler horizontally on the sample, measure 10cm (4in) across and mark with a pin at each end. Count the number of stitches between the pins. To check the row tension (gauge), place a ruler vertically on the sample, measure 10cm (4in) and mark with pins. Count the number of rows between the pins. If the number of stitches and rows is greater than specified in the pattern, make a new swatch using larger needles; if it is less, make a new swatch using smaller needles.

MAKING A SLIP KNOT

A slip knot is the basis of all casting-on techniques and is therefore the starting point for almost everything you do in knitting and crochet.

1

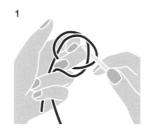

1 Wind the yarn around two fingers twice as shown. Insert a knitting needle through the first (front) strand and under the second (back) one.

2

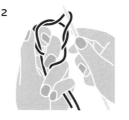

2 Using the needle, pull the back strand through the front one to form a loop.

3

3 Holding the loose ends of the yarn with your left hand, pull the needle upwards, thus tightening the knot. Pull the ball end of the yarn again to tighten the knot further.

CASTING ON

'Casting on' is the term used for making a row of stitches to be used as a foundation for your knitting.

THE BASIC STITCHES

Knit and purl stitches form the basis of all knitted fabrics. The knit stitch is the easiest to learn and once you have mastered this you can move on to the purl stitch, which is the reverse of the knit stitch.

1

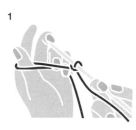

1 Make a slip knot 100cm (40in) from the end of the yarn. Hold the needle in your right hand with the ball end of the yarn over your index finger. *Wind the loose end of the yarn around your left thumb from front to back.

2

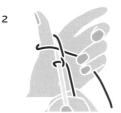

2 Insert the point of the needle under the first strand of yarn on your thumb.

3 With your right index finger, take the ball end of the yarn over the point of the needle.

3

4 Pull a loop through to form the first stitch. Remove your left thumb from the yarn. Pull the loose end to secure the stitch. Repeat from * until the required number of stitches have been cast on.

4

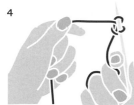

KNIT STITCH

1

1 Hold the needle with the cast-on stitches in your left hand, with the loose yarn at the back of the work. Insert the right-hand needle from left to right through the front of the first stitch on the left-hand needle.

2

2 Wrap the yarn from left to right over the point of the right-hand needle.

3 Draw the yarn through the stitch, thus forming a new stitch on the right-hand needle.

3

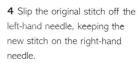

4 Slip the original stitch off the left-hand needle, keeping the new stitch on the right-hand needle.

5 To knit a row, repeat steps 1 to 4 until all the stitches have been transferred from the left-hand needle to the right-hand needle. Turn the work, transferring the needle with the stitches to your left hand to work the next row.

4

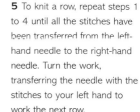

PURL STITCH

1 Hold the needle with the stitches in your left hand, with the loose yarn at the front of the work. Insert the right-hand needle from right to left into the front of the first stitch on the left-hand needle.

2 Wrap the yarn from right to left, up and over the point of the right-hand needle.

3 Draw the yarn through the stitch, thus forming a new stitch on the right-hand needle.

4 Slip the original stitch off the left-hand needle, keeping the new stitch on the right-hand needle.

5 To purl a row, repeat steps 1 to 4 until all the stitches have been transferred from the left-hand needle to the right-hand needle. Turn the work, transferring the needle with the stitches to your left hand to work the next row.

INCREASING AND DECREASING

Many projects will require some shaping, either just to add interest or to make the various sections fit together properly. Shaping is achieved by increasing or decreasing the number of stitches you are working.

INCREASING

The simplest method of increasing one stitch is to work into the front and back of the same stitch.

On a knit row, knit into the front of the stitch to be increased, then before slipping it off the needle, place the right-hand needle behind the left-hand one and knit again into the back of it (inc). Slip the original stitch off the left-hand needle. On a purl row, purl into the front of the stitch to be increased, then before slipping it off the needle, purl again into the back of it. Slip the original stitch off the left-hand needle.

DECREASING

The simplest method of decreasing one stitch is to work two stitches together.

On a knit row, insert the right-hand needle from left to right through two stitches instead of one, then knit them together as one stitch. This is called knit two together (k2tog).

On a purl row, insert the right-hand needle from right to left through two stitches instead of one, then purl them together as one stitch. This is called purl two together (p2tog).

INTARSIA STITCHES

'Intarsia' is where the pattern is worked in large blocks of colour at a time, requiring a separate ball of yarn for each area of colour.

DIAGONAL COLOUR CHANGE WITH A SLANT TO THE LEFT

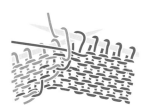

On a wrong-side row, with the yarns at the front of the work, take the first colour over the second colour, drop it, then pick up the second colour underneath the first colour, thus crossing the two colours over one another.

DIAGONAL COLOUR CHANGE WITH A SLANT TO THE RIGHT

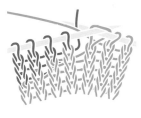

On a right-side row, with the yarns at the back of the work, take the first colour over the second colour, drop it, then pick up the second colour underneath the first colour, thus crossing the two colours.

VERTICAL COLOUR CHANGE

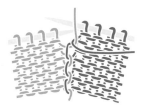

Work in the first colour to the colour change, then drop the first colour, pick up the second colour underneath the first colour, crossing the two colours over before working the next stitch in the second colour. After a colour change, work the first stitch firmly to prevent a gap forming between colours.

FAIR ISLE STITCHES

Yarn that is not in use is left at the back of the work until needed. The loops formed by this are called 'floats' and it is important that they are not pulled too tightly when working the next stitch, as this will pull your knitting.

1  **2**  **3** 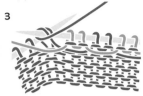 **4**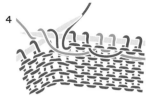

1 On a knit row, hold the first colour in your right hand and the second colour in your left hand. Knit the required number of stitches as usual with the first colour, carrying the second colour loosely across the wrong side of the work.

2 To knit a stitch in the second colour, insert the right-hand needle into the next stitch, then draw a loop through from the yarn held in the left hand, carrying the yarn in the right hand loosely across the wrong side until required.

3 On a purl row, hold the yarns as for the knit rows. Purl the required number of stitches as usual with the first colour, carrying the second colour loosely across these stitches on the wrong side of the work.

4 To purl a stitch in the second colour, insert the right-hand needle into the next stitch, then draw a loop through from the yarn held in the left hand, carrying the yarn in the right hand loosely across the wrong side until next required.

CASTING (BINDING) OFF

This is the most commonly used method of securing stitches at the end of a piece of knitting. The cast-off edge should have the same 'give' or elasticity as the fabric; cast (bind) off in the stitch used for the main fabric unless the pattern directs otherwise.

KNITWISE

Knit two stitches. *Using the point of the left-hand needle, lift the first stitch on the right-hand needle over the second, then drop it off the needle. Knit the next stitch and repeat from * until all stitches have been worked off the left-hand needle and only one stitch remains on the right-hand needle. Cut the yarn, leaving enough to sew in the end. Thread the end through the stitch, then slip it off the needle. Draw the yarn up firmly to fasten off.

PURLWISE

Purl two stitches. *Using the point of the left-hand needle, lift the first stitch on the right-hand needle over the second and drop it off the needle. Purl the next stitch and repeat from * until all the stitches have been worked off the left-hand needle and only one stitch remains on the right-hand needle. Cut the yarn, leaving enough to sew in the end. Thread the end through the stitch, then slip it off the needle. Draw the yarn up firmly to fasten off.

Crochet

TENSION (GAUGE)

This is the number of rows and stitches per centimetre or inch, usually measured over a 10cm (4in) square. The tension (gauge) will determine the size of the finished item. The correct tension (gauge) is given at the beginning of each pattern. Crochet a small swatch, using the recommended yarn and hook, to make sure you are working to the correct tension (gauge). If your work is too loose, choose a hook that is one size smaller, and if it is too tight, choose a hook the next size up. When making clothes, it is important to check tension (gauge) before you start; it is not worth making something the wrong size. When measuring work, lay it on a flat surface and always measure at the centre, rather than at the side edges.

- -

BASIC STITCHES

Start by making a series of chains – around 10 will be enough. Now you're ready to practise the following stitches.

SLIP STITCH (SS) (SL ST)

1 This is the shortest stitch and mostly used for joining and shaping. Insert the hook into a stitch or chain (always remember to insert the hook under both strands of the stitch), yarn over the hook from the back to the front of the hook, and draw the hook through the stitch and the loop on the hook. You are left with just 1 loop on the hook. This is 1 slip stitch.

DOUBLE CROCHET (DC)
(SINGLE CROCHET (SC))

1 Insert the hook into the second chain from the hook, yarn over the hook, draw the loop through your work.

2 Yarn over and draw the hook through both loops on the hook; 1 loop on the hook. This is 1 double crochet.

3 Repeat into the next stitch or chain until you've reached the end of the row, make 1 chain stitch – this is your turning chain – turn the work and work 1 double crochet (single crochet) into each stitch of the previous row, ensuring that you insert the hook under both loops of the stitch you are crocheting into.

HALF TREBLE CROCHET (HTR)
(HALF DOUBLE CROCHET (HDC))

1 Yarn over the hook before inserting the hook into the third chain from the hook, yarn over, draw 1 loop through the work, yarn over, draw through all 3 loops on the hook; 1 loop on the hook. This is 1 half treble crochet (half double crochet).

2 When you reach the end of the row, make 2 chains – this counts as the first stitch of the next row. Turn the work, skip the first half treble crochet (half double crochet) of the previous row and insert the hook into the second stitch of the new row. Continue to work until the end of the row. At the end of the row, work the last half treble (half double) into the top of the turning chain of the row below.

TREBLE CROCHET (TR)
(DOUBLE CROCHET (DC)

1 Start by wrapping the yarn over the hook and insert the hook into the fourth chain from the hook, yarn over, draw 1 loop through the work

2 Yarn over, draw through the first 2 loops on the hook, yarn over, draw through the remaining 2 loops on the hook; 1 loop on the hook. This is 1 treble crochet (double crochet).

3 When you reach the end of the row, make 3 chains. These count as the first stitch of the next row. Turn the work and skip the first treble crochet (double crochet) of the previous row; insert the hook into the second stitch of the new row. Continue to work until the end of the row, inserting the last treble crochet (double crochet) into the top of the turning chain of the row below.

BASIC TECHNIQUES

As well as working from right to left in rows, crochet can also be worked in a circular fashion (referred to as working in the round), or even in a continuous spiral to make seamless items such as hats, bags and other rounded objects.

MAKING FABRIC – WORKING IN ROWS

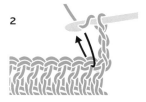

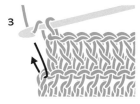

1 Make as many chain stitches as you require. This row is called the base chain. Insert the hook into the second chain from the hook (not counting the chain on the hook) for double crochet (single crochet), third chain from the hook for treble crochet (double crochet)

2 Work from right to left, inserting the hook under two of the three threads in each chain.

3 When you reach the end of the row, work one or more turning chains, depending on the height of the stitch.

Turning chains should be worked as follows:
Double (single) crochet: 1 chain.
Half treble (half double): 2 chains.
Treble (double): 3 chains.
Double treble (treble): 4 chains.
Triple treble (double treble): 5 chains.

Now turn the work to begin working on the next row (remember always to turn your work in the same direction). When working in double crochet (single crochet), insert the hook into the first stitch in the new row and work each stitch to the end of the row, excluding the turning chain. For all other stitches, unless the pattern states otherwise, the turning chain counts as the first stitch. Skip 1 stitch and work each stitch to the end of the row, including the top of the turning chain.

MAKING FABRIC – WORKING IN THE ROUND

1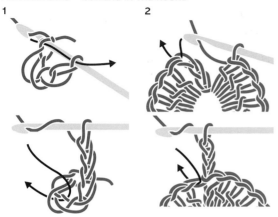

2

1 Crochet in the round starts with a ring. To make a ring, make a series of chains and join the last chain to the first with a slip stitch.

2 To make the first round, work a starting chain to the height of the stitch you are working in. Then work as many stitches as you need into the centre of the ring and finish the round with a slip stitch into the first stitch.

3 Begin the second and subsequent rounds with a starting chain (worked the same way as a turning chain, with the number of chains depending on the stitch you are working: see page 92). Then insert the hook under the top 2 loops of each stitch in the previous round. At the end of the round, join to the top of the starting chain with a slip stitch, as in step 2.

INCREASING   ## DECREASING

As with knitting, fabric is often shaped by increasing the number of stitches in a row or round. To increase, simply work an additional stitch into the next stitch. A single increase is made by working 2 stitches into the same stitch. You can of course increase by more than 1 stitch at a time.

DC2TOG
To decrease 1 stitch in double crochet (dc2tog) (single crochet (sc2tog)), insert hook into next stitch, yarn over, draw through the work, insert hook into the next stitch, yarn over, draw through the work, yarn over, draw through all 3 loops, leaving just 1 loop on the hook.

DC3TOG
To decrease by 2 stitches in double crochet (single crochet), work 3 stitches together, dc3tog (sc3tog), by working as for dc2tog (sc2tog) until you have 3 loops on the hook. Insert the hook into the next stitch, yarn over, draw through the work, yarn over and draw through all 4 loops.

TR2TOG
To decrease 1 stitch in treble crochet (tr2tog) (double crochet (dc2tog)), yarn over, insert hook into next stitch, yarn over, draw through work, yarn over, draw through 2 loops, yarn over, insert hook into next stitch, yarn over, draw through work, yarn over, draw through 2 loops, yarn over, draw through all 3 loops.

FINISHING OFF

Once you have fastened off, this is a useful way of sewing up crochet seams.

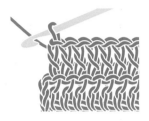 

FASTENING OFF

Cut the yarn, leaving roughly 13cm (5in). Make 1 chain and draw the tail through the chain and pull firmly. Weave the end a few centimetres or an inch in one direction and then back the other way for a neat and secure finish.

FLAT STITCH

This seam creates an almost invisible join. Lay the two sections right-side up, with the stitches aligned. Using a tapestry needle, insert under the lower half of the edge stitch on one section, then under the upper half of the edge stitch on the opposite section.

Abbreviations

KNITTING ABBREVIATIONS

alt = alternate/alternating
beg = beginning
cont = continue
dec = decrease
dpn = double-pointed needle
foll = following
inc = increase/increasing
k= knit
k2tog = knit two together
LH = left-hand
m1 = make one st. Lift the horizontal strand between the st just worked and next st, then knit through back of this thread.
p = purl
p2tog = purl two together
patt = pattern
prev = previous
psso = pass slipped stitch over
rem = remaining
rep = repeat
Rev st st = reverse stocking (stockinette) stitch
RH = right-hand
RS = right side
sl = slip
skpo = slip 1 st knitwise, knit 1 st, pass slipped stitch over
St st = stocking (stockinette) stitch
st(s) = stitch(es)

tog = together
TS = thumb section
tbl = through back of loops
WS = wrong side
yfwd = yarn forward
yon = yarn over needle
yrn = yarn around needle

CROCHET ABBREVIATIONS

ch = chain
cluster = [yoh and insert hook as indicated, yoh and draw loops through, yoh and draw through first loop, yoh and draw through 2 loops] twice, yoh and draw through all 3 loops on hook
dc = double crochet
dtr = double treble
htr = half treble
sc = single crochet
sp(s) = space(s)
ss = slip stitch
tr = treble
tr tr = triple treble
tr3tog = [yoh and insert hook as indicated, yoh and draw loop through, yoh and draw through 2 loops] 3 times, yoh and draw through all 4 loops on hook

tr5tog = [yoh and insert hook as indicated, yoh and draw loop through, yoh and draw through 2 loops] 5 times, yoh and draw through all 6 loops on hook

qtr = quintuple treble. [yoh] 5 times, insert hook as indicated, yoh and draw loop through, [yoh and draw through 2 loops] 6 times

yoh = yarn over hook

SPECIAL ABBREVIATIONS

CHEVRON BAG

tr3tog = [yoh and insert hook as indicated, yoh and draw loop through, yoh and draw through 2 loops] 3 times, yoh and draw through all 4 loops on hook

tr5tog = [yoh and insert hook as indicated, yoh and draw loop through, yoh and draw through 2 loops] 5 times, yoh and draw through all 6 loops on hook

TWEEDY SHOPPER

tr3tog = [yoh and insert hook as indicated, yoh and draw loop through, yoh and draw through 2 loops] 3 times, yoh and draw through all 4 loops on hook

UBER BAG

qtr = quintuple treble worked as follows: [yoh] 5 times, insert hook as indicated, yoh and draw loop through, [yoh and draw through 2 loops] 6 times

CLUSTER BEACH BAG

cluster = [yoh and insert hook as indicated, yoh and draw loops through, yoh and draw through first loop, yoh and draw through 2 loops] twice, yoh and draw through all 3 loops on hook

SEWING SEAMS

You can use ordinary backstitch to sew up bag seams. This is the most suitable stitch if you are sewing a circular base into a bag or sewing two different-shaped edges together.
If you are sewing a straight seam, then mattress stitch works well.
Lay the pieces right side up and next to each other. You are going to work up the side of the knitted pieces between the edge stitch and the next stitch, the edge stitch from each side will dissapear into the seam. Put the tapestry needle in between the edge and next stitch on one knitted piece and take it up the coloumn between the edge stitch and next stitch, going under two stitch bars.. Move over to the other piece and do the same. Go back to the point where the needle came out on the first piece and put it back in, going up the column under the next two bars. Continue going back and forth and pulling the thread tight each time. You will see that the two edges are pulled together.

SEWING IN ENDS

Once your garment has been sewn together the yarn ends need to be sewn into the seams. Once at a time, thread the yarn ends into a tapestry needle and weave them into the seam. Cut off the end of the yarn.

KITCHENER STITCH

With the stitches on two parallel, double-pointed needles, make sure that the working yarn is coming from the back needle. Take the tapestry needle through the first stitch on the front needle as if to purl and leave the stitch on the needle. Next, go through the first stitch on the back needle as if to knit – leave this stitch on the needle. Keeping the working yarn below the needles, work 2 sts on the front needle, followed by 2 sts on the back needle across the row as follows:
On front needle, go through the first st as if to knit and drop it off the needle. Go through the second st as if to knit and leave it on the needle. Tighten the yarn. On the back needle, go through the first st as if to purl and drop it off the needle. Go through second st as if to knit and leave it on the needle. Tighten the yarn. When there is only one stitch on one needle, go through the front stitch as if to drop it off the needle. Go through the back stitch as if to purl and drop it off the needle. Pull the tail to the inside and weave in.

Resources

Alchemy
PO Box 1080
Sebastopol
CA 95473
USA
+1 707 823 3276
www.alchemyyarns.com

Coats
PO Box 22
Lingfield House
Lingfield Point
McMullen Road
Darlington
County Durham DL1 1YQ
England, United Kingdom
01325 394237
www.coatscrafts.co.uk

Debbie Bliss Yarns
c/o Designer Yarns Ltd.
Unit 8-10 Newbridge
Industrial Estate
Pitt Street
Keighley
West Yorkshire
BD21 4PQ
01535 664222
www.designeryarns.uk.com

GGH
Mühlenstraße 74
25421 Pinneberg
Germany
+49 (0)4101 208484
www.ggh-garn.de

Jamieson & Smith Ltd
90 North Road
Lerwick
Shetland Islands
ZE1 0PQ
01595 693579
www.jamiesonandsmith.co.uk

Louisa Harding
See Debbie Bliss

Rowan Yarns
Green Lane Mill
Holmfirth HD9 2BR
01484 681881
www.knitrowan.com

Rowan Yarn Classics
Green Lane Mill
Holmfirth HD9 2BR
01484 681881
www.ryclassic.com

Twilley's
c/o Angel Yarns
Angel House
77 North Street
Portslade
East Sussex
BN41 1DZ
0870 766 6212
www.angelyarns.com

Love crafts? Crafters, keep updated on all exciting news from Collins & Brown. Email **lovecrafts@anovabooks.com** to register for free email alerts and author events.